OSH INDUCTION PROGRAM IN ENHANCING SAFETY AWARENESS AMONGST FABRICATION WORKERS IN BROOKE DOCKYARD, KUCHING, SARAWAK

Osh Induction Program in Enhancing Safety Awareness Amongst Fabrication Workers in Brooke Dockyard, Kuching, Sarawak

Andrew Anak Ronggie

PARTRIDGE
A Penguin Random House Company

To order additional copies of this book, contact
Toll Free 800 101 2657 (Singapore)
Toll Free 1 800 81 7340 (Malaysia)
orders.singapore@partridgepublishing.com

www.partridgepublishing.com/singapore

Contents

Chapter 1

INTRODUCTION

1.1 Introduction to the OSH Program

In order to create a safe and healthy working environment in the fabrication and engineering work industry, an efficient and appropriate system of safety and health is of considerable importance. To investigate, learn, and improve the system of safety and health in these industries, the adoption of an effective occupational safety and health (OSH) management system is required to show how the industries manage safety and health and mitigate incidents or injuries at the workplace. The approach of managing OSH in a systematic way through the adoption of relevant and effective OSH management system in various industries has become increasingly popular in recent years.

The aim of this study is to examine the knowledge and awareness level among employees regarding safety and health at a selected fabrication yard and to ensure that the Occupational Safety and Health Act of 1994 and its regulations are followed by the industries. This is in line with the objective of promoting a safe and healthy working environment and a culture of safety among employees.

The fabrication yard, namely Brooke Dockyard, provides training widely across the organization, from the top management level to the general worker. However, enforcement depends on the competency requirements involved.

Table 1.1: OSH training matrix.

Job Description	Offshore Safety Client (1)	Offshore Safety Client (2)	Basic Survival at Sea (3)	Basic Fire Fighting	Industrial First-Aid & CPR	Breath Apparatus Training	Supervising HSE Training	Welding & Hot work Safety	Scaffolding Safety Training	Rigging & Slinging Safety	HUET (4)	U-See-U Act Training	PLC Session	Work Place LSR Session
	1	2	3	4	5	6	7	8	9	10	11	12	13	14
Construction/ Maintenance														
CEO/General Manager	R	M	R	NR	NR	NR	NR	NR	NR	NR	R	R	M	M
Senior Manager/ Manager	M	M	R	M	R	R	M	R	R	R	R	M	M	M
Superintendent/ Coordinator	M	M	R	M	R	R	M	R	R	R	R	M	M	M
Engineer	M	M	M	M	M	M	M	M	M	R	M	M	M	M
Supervisor/ Inspector	M	M	M	M	M	M	M	M	M	M	M	M	M	M
HSE Professional/ Advisor	M	M	M	M	M	M	M	M	M	M	M	M	M	M
Electrician	M	M	M	R	M	R	R	R	NR	NR	M	M	M	M
Fitter	M	M	M	R	R	R	NR	R	R	M	M	M	M	M

Welder	M	M	M	M	R	R	NR	M	R	NR	M	M	M	M
Rigger/ Crane Operator	M	M	M	R	R	R	NR	R	R	M	M	M	M	M
Technician	M	M	M	R	R	R	NR	R	R	R	M	M	M	M
Mechanic	M	M	M	R	R	R	NR	R	R	R	M	M	M	M
Scaffolder	M	M	M	R	R	R	NR	NR	M	R	M	M	M	M
Painter	M	M	M	R	R	R	NR	R	R	R	M	M	M	M
Plumber	M	M	M	R	R	R	NR	R	R	R	M	M	M	M
Insulator	M	M	M	R	R	R	NR	R	R	R	M	M	M	M
General Worker	M	M	M	R	R	R	NR	R	R	R	M	M	M	M

Table 1.1: OSH training matrix (Continue).

Job Description	Modern HSE Management Course	Combustible Compressed Gas Safety	Hearts & Minds	Electrical Safety	Scaffolding Inspection	Task Observation & Job Safety Analysis	Internal Safety Auditing	Professional Accident Inspection	Professional Accident Inspection	Radiation Safety	Life Saving Rules Induction	CIDB Induction	NIOSP Induction
	15	16	17	18	19	20	21	22	23	24	25	26	27
Construction/ Maintenance													
CEO/General Manager	M	R	M	R	R	R	R	R	R	R	M	M	M
Senior Manager/ Manager	M	R	M	R	R	M	M	M	R	R	M	M	M
Superintendent/ Coordinator	M	R	M	R	R	M	M	M	M	M	M	M	M
Engineer	M	M	M	M	M	M	M	M	M	M	M	M	M
Supervisor/ Inspector	R	M	M	M	M	M	M	M	M	M	M	M	M
HSE Professional/ Advisor	R	M	M	M	M	M	M	M	M	M	M	M	M
Electrician	NR	M	R	R	M	R	NR	NR	R	R	M	M	M
Fitter	NR	M	R	R	R	R	NR	NR	R	M	M	M	M

Welder	NR	M	R	M	R	R	NR	NR	R	R	M	M	M
Rigger/ Crane Operator	NR	R	R	R	R	R	NR	NR	M	M	M	M	M
Technician	NR	R	R	R	R	R	NR	NR	NR	NR	M	M	M
Mechanic	NR	R	R	R	R	R	NR	NR	R	R	M	M	M
Scaffolder	NR	R	R	R	R	R	NR	NR	R	R	M	M	M
Painter	NR	R	R	R	R	R	NR	NR	R	NR	M	M	M
Plumber	NR	R	R	R	R	R	NR	NR	NR	NR	M	M	M
Insulator	NR	R	R	R	R	R	NR	NR	R	R	M	M	M
General Worker	NR	M	R	R	R	R	NR	NR	R	R	M	M	M
LEGEND:	M	Mandatory											

1.2 Background of Brooke Dockyard

Brooke Dockyard was established in 1912 during the reign of the second White Rajah of Sarawak, Charles Brooke. It underwent a few rounds of organizational restructuring until, in 1977, Brooke Dockyard became a fully owned government statutory body under the BDEWC Ordinance (Cap. 100). Brooke Dockyard and Engineering Works Corporation, a name synonymous with the heritage and culture of Sarawak, was the oldest shipyard in Malaysia. Brooke Dockyard now has firmly established itself as a leading marine-engineering entity in Sarawak with active involvement in the oil and gas, shipbuilding, ship repair, bridges infrastructure, and onshore-manufacturing sectors. It has a steady workforce of more than four hundred personnel, with its competencies ranging from engineering to welding and maintenance services.

Brooke Dockyard is a government statutory body fully owned by the state government of Sarawak under the Ministry of Infrastructure Development and Communications. It has been providing employment for the people of Sarawak for more than one hundred years, and it has been dealing in the repairs of government vessels and machineries as well as servicing private vessels. Brooke Dockyard started as a major offshore modules fabricator in 1996 and has accomplished more than twenty offshore modules and four offshore living quarters and twelve substructures. Since then, other successes have included building the navigational boats, multi-mission vessels, ferries for marine-engineering works, and steel-arch bridges, in an effort to be a major service provider in the petroleum, marine, and manufacturing industries.

Currently, Brooke Dockyard and Engineering Works Corporation (BDEWC) is an integrated engineering corporation building customized products with no compromise on the standards of safety and quality. The quality management system is accredited to ISO 9001:2000 in 1999 and upgraded to ISO 9001:2008 in 2010 by Lloyds Register in shipbuilding up to 2,500 DWT and fabrication of structural assemblies and modules for the oil and gas industries, assessed and acknowledged by our reputable clients through external audits. Brooke Dockyard now has a proper protocol of Quality Manual and QA/QC Procedures to support project execution works.

Vision

To be the preferred global engineering and construction service provider in petroleum, marine, and manufacturing industries.

Mission

To provide quality products and services in a competitive and innovative manner to the satisfaction of our stakeholders, with the aim to provide total solutions for customized products in our identified industries.

Competency Statement

To provide total solutions for customized products in identified and established industries.

HSE Safety Achievements

The HSE policy is, "Safety comes first and zero-time incident (LTI)." Safety is the driving culture of the corporation. No compromises have been made to ensure Brooke Dockyard is a safe place for people to work, not only for themselves but for their families. Brooke Dockyard has been rated at level 3.2 (Dec. 2010) for Shell HSE Management System. In 2000 and 2001, Brooke Dockyard was named the Malaysian Company in Safety Performance by Petronas. Other awards include:

➢ Gold award in the Project Fabrication category for 2000–2001 from Petronas for HSE Management System Fabrication Contractor category.

➢ Health & Safety Environment Award from Sarawak Shell Malaysia for the completion of SFJT-C Fabrication and Topsides without LTI in 2001.

➢ Certificate of Achievement from Murphy Sarawak Oil for the completion of WP-IA Topsides.

➢ Murphy Safety Award for the achievement of 250,000 work hours with no lost-time incidents for the Fabrication of West Patricia Production A Platform in March 2004.

➢ CIDB Five-Star SHASSICS Assessment for Fabrication of St. Joseph GRS Living Quarters, Topsides, and Substructure for Sabah Shell Petroleum Company in 2010.

➢ Malaysian Construction Industry Excellence Award in Safety and Health Category in 2011.

HSE Accreditation

Brooke Dockyard is certified in OHSAS 18001:2007 OSH Management System for Fabrication of Structural Assemblies and Modules for Oil & Gas Industries and the construction of ships up to 2,500 DWT by SIRIM QAS International Sdn. Bhd. and IQ Net International in October 2009 and recertified in 2012 with a validity of 3 years until October 2015. Brooke Dockyard achieved second HSE milestones of 800,000 man-hours without lost-time incidents (LTI) for St. Joseph Redevelopment Project on March 19, 2010, as shown in figure 1.1.

Figure 1.1: HSE Manager, Mr. Andrew Ronggie, receiving certificate of appreciation.

Supported by tables 1.2 and 1.3, which indicate data on incidents at the workplace.

Table 1.2: Data on injuries in the workplace (2009–2014, and as of December 2014).

TYPE OF INCIDENTS \ YEAR	2009	2010	2011	2012	2013	2014
1. LOST TIME INCIDENT (LTI)						
1.1 No. of Fatality	0	0	0	0	0	0
1.2 No. of Permanent Total Disability (PTD)	0	0	0	0	0	0
1.3No. of Permanent Partial Disability (PPD)	0	0	0	0	0	0
1.4 No. of Lost Work Day Case	0	0	0	0	0	0
2. INJURIOUS NON-LTI						
2.1No. of Restricted Workday Case (RWC)	1 (see note 3)	0	0	0	0	0
2.2 No. of Medical Treatment Case (MTC)	0	0	0	2	2	0
2.3 No. of First Aid Case (FAC)	0	0	1	0	2	0
2.4 No. of Occupational Illness /Incident	1 (see note 2)	0	1	0	0	0
3. NON-INJURIOUS						
3.1 No. of Major Fire/Explosion	0	0	0	0	0	0
3.2 No. of Property Damage / Loss	0	3	3	0	0	0
3.3 No. of Vehicle Incident (work site)	0	0	0	0	0	0
3.4 No. of Oil Spill < 5 BBLS	0	0	0	0	0	0
3.5 No. of Oil Spill > 5 BBLS	0	0	0	0	0	0
4. INCIDENT						
4.1 Near Misses	1	0	0	0	1	0

5. U-See U-Act Program					
5.1 No. of Unsafe Act findings	148	516	218	83	2,163	425
5.2 No. of Unsafe Condition findings	669	2,011	563	272		
6. LTI Frequency Rate	0	0	0	0	0	0
7. LTI Severity Rate	0	0	0	0	0	0
Total Recordable Cum. Freq. Rate (TRCF)	2.18	0	0	1.92	1.05	0
No. of Emergency /Fire Drill	1	1	1	2	3	3
	2	2	2	2	0	0
No. of HSE Audit (Internal/external	2	3	2	2	2	4
No. of NC to HSE applicable laws/ regulations	0	0	0	0	0	0
Total Man-hours Worked LTI Free	456,652	1,682,570	587,200	1,042,823	1,896,683	1,225,922
Projects undertaken	B11LQ &SJRD	SJRD, MRU, & Belum & Pem	Belum & Pemanis, MEPA	MEPA & S.Acis	South Acis	S. Acis & SASA
Manhour cumulative for year to date (since 1997)	8,941,582	10,624,152	11,211,352	12,254,175	14,150,858	15,897,740

Note:
1. On 22/4/2009, Medevac for HUC personnel from workboat at B11LQ to Miri Hospital due to musculoskeletal pain. Categorised as Occupational Illness.
2. On 26/10/2009, dust entered right eye of grinder while adjusting it exhaust fan blower. Sent to eye specialist for treatment. Categorised as RWC.
3. Property Damage. One on 17/5/10 -Vehicle Damage & 30/6/2010 - UPS Battery Cells Damaged & Scaffolding Damage, forklift battery overheated, inbalanced ball valve fell over & minor damage.
4. On 21/4/2011, 11 subcontractor personnel experienced mild food poisoning on board Installation Barge. Categorised as Occupational Illness (OI)
5. MTC# 1 on 26/6/12-Worker injured tip of little finger when pinched by shifted beam. MTC#2: 26/12/12-Grinder adjusted handglove and lost control grinding machine caused minor laceration to his thigh.
6. MTC#1 on 23/6/13 Rigger fell from height. MTC#2 on 16/8/13 when Rigger hit by shifted object.
7. Total Manhours worked since 1997 as cut - of. March 2014 : 14,707,458
8. Total Manhours worked since last Lost Time Incident (LTI) in 2007 : 8,593,960

Table 1.3: Incident rate for the last five years and year to date (December 31, 2014).

No. of Injury/ Year	2009	2010	2011	2012	2013	2014
No of Injury	1	0	0	2	2	0
Manhours worked	456,652	1,682,570	587,200	1,042,823	1,896,683	1,225,922
Incident Rate	0.438	0	0	0.38	0.21	0
Total Recordable Cumulative Frequency Rate	2.18	0	0	1.92	1.05	0

Using the formulae:

1. Incident Rate, IR = (N/H) x 200,00
   Where, N is total no. of incident
   H is the total no. of hours by the employees during the year.

2. Total Recordable Cumulative Frequency, TRCF
   TRCF = Total LTI + RWC + MTC / (Total Manhours Worked) x 1,000,000 Manhours.

1.3 Problem Statement

Every year, there are about 270 million occupational accidents and 160 million occupational diseases globally. Of these, about 360,000 accidents and 1.6 million diseases are fatal. Thus, about 2 million citizens of the world will die because of occupational safety and health reasons; 90 percent of this occurs in developing countries (Pearce et al. 2002).

There are some fifty major occupational diseases listed in official lists and textbooks of occupational medicine (WHO 1995). Many of the industrialized countries see declining morbidity in such traditional diseases as chemical poisonings, pneumoconiosis, vibration-induced vasospastic syndrome, or noise-induced hearing loss, while work-related diseases increase in occurrence (WHO 1989). Some of the old diseases, such as asbestos-related cancers, however, will continue to increase still for two to three decades (Doll and Peto 1981).

In addition to traditional occupational health problems, a number of new problems will also be met with a totally new character and often with a multifactorial and multicausal origin. Instead of a search for specific diseases, concern will be focused increasingly on functional capacity and behavioral, environmental, and social determinants of work ability, work motivation, and the quality of working life in general. Hence, focus on health problems and new aspects, such as productivity, quality of products, innovation, capacity to handle clients, and lifelong work ability, are being given growing attention. These outcomes are often ill defined and cannot necessarily be measured with existing methods.

The inter-individual variation in outcomes may be wide and confounded by several new factors either at work or outside of work. The outcomes, such as the reduction of functional capacity or work ability, can also be very context dependent. A typical example is the work ability index (WAI), which is dependent on both the capacity of the worker and the demands of the job (Ilmarinen et al. 1978). Another example is the risk of burnout, which is highly dependent on the person's resources, but also on the context of work and on several factors occurring at the workplace. Such a new development calls for a qualitative research approach to complement the quantitative one.

Occupational safety and health is the discipline concerned with preserving and protecting human and facility resources in the workplace. Nowadays, we often hear of accidents in manufacturing industries. The percentages of an accident in the manufacturing industries sector are always high compared to the other sectors. These accidents happen because of poor or apathetic attitudes regarding occupational safety and health (OSH) performances in some companies. OSH standards are mandatory rules and standards set and enforced to eliminate or reduce OSH hazards in the workplace. OSH standards aim to provide at least the minimum acceptable degree of protection that must be afforded to every worker in relation to the working conditions and dangers of injury, sickness, or death that may arise by reason of an employee's occupation.

1.4 Objective of Study

There are two objectives formulated to answer the research questions for this study, such as:

- ➢ to determine the level of OSH knowledge and awareness among the employees; and
- ➢ to identify the effectiveness of an OSH training program in relating to mitigate injuries among employees in workplaces.

1.5 Hypotheses of the Study

These hypotheses examine the in-depth analysis between variables by using empirical statistics. The proposed hypotheses and units of analysis for this study are shown in table 1.4.

Table 1.4. Study's hypotheses and unit of analysis.

Hypotheses	Analysis
H_{01}: There is no significant relationship between levels of OSH knowledge and awareness by workers with a demographic background. • Age group • Educational level • Ethnicity • Gender • Job title • Number of years' experience • Attended the induction course on OSH • Accident in the workplace	Pearson's Coefficient Pearson's Coefficient Pearson's Coefficient T-Test Pearson's Coefficient Pearson's Coefficient Pearson's Coefficient Pearson's Coefficient
H_{02}: There is no significant relationship between levels of OSH knowledge by workers with perception on organization safety management in the organization.	One-Way ANOVA
H_{03}: There is no significant relationship between levels of OSH knowledge by workers with safety program policies in the organization.	One-Way ANOVA
H_{04}: There is no significant relationship between levels of OSH knowledge by workers with perception on safety behavior in the workplace in the organization.	One-Way ANOVA

1.6 Significance of the Study

This study looks in to the effectiveness of the training programs and the level of safety awareness on metal fabrication works. The study will look into the selected groups of workers:

those who had attended the OSH training program and work in a safe environment. The scope does not look in to the formulation of policies and regulations but serves as a mere enlightenment toward further improvement on safety and healthy working environments in Brooke Dockyards.

1.7 Chapter Summary

This chapter has outlined the background, the problem statement, and the objectives of the study. In addition, it has also elaborated the conceptual framework of the study. Included in the discussion of this chapter was the significance of the study. Chapter 2 will further dwell on the literature review.

Chapter 2

LITERATURE REVIEW

2.1 Introduction

This chapter focuses on the literature review regarding the perception on quality of life among patients with hyperthyroid disease. This section reviews the concept of the study, while the last section discusses some of the major research findings on the subject that has been conducted.

2.2 OSH Management

Previous studies (Bottani, Monica, and Vignali 2009) have demonstrated that effective safety management improves the level of safety in an organization and thus can be seen to decrease damages and harm from incidents. *Safety management* refers to the tangible practices, responsibility, and performance related to safety (cited from Mearns, Whitaker, and Flin 2003). Mearns (et al. 2003) noted some common themes of safety management practices: management commitment to safety, safety communication, health and safety objectives, training needs, rewarding performance, and worker involvement. They also maintained the associations between safety management, safety climate, and safety culture. *Safety climate* is considered to be the precise indicator of overall safety culture, while safety management practices display the safety culture of top management, and as a result, good safety management practices are reflected in enhanced safety climate of all employees. The terms *culture* and *climate* have been used interchangeably in the literature to reveal employees' attitudes toward safety (Glendon and Stanton 2000; HSE 2002). HSE defined *safety climate* as "the attitudes in relation to safety within an organization." Hale described *safety culture* as "the attitudes, beliefs, and perceptions shared by natural groups as defining norms and values, which determine how they react in relation to risks and risk control systems."

A study conducted (Hsu, Lee, Wu, and Takano 2007) on organizational factors on safety in Taiwan and Japan reported that the influence of organizational factors in both countries were different because of dissimilar culture. For example, they discovered that Taiwanese leadership style was "top-down directive," where top management communicated safety policies and involved in safety activities, while Japanese safety leadership was more focused on "bottom-up participative," where top management promoted employees' participation in any safety activities.

Besides leadership style, Marsh (et al. 1995) noted that management commitment plays a vital role in all aspects of safety intervention. Management commitment to safety indicates the extent to which the organization's top management demonstrates positive and supportive safety attitudes toward their employees' safety (Hsu et al. 2007). From a prior study, Yule, Flin and Murdy (2007) noted that employees' perception of dedicated management's actions toward safety had resulted in accident reduction. The Occupational Safety and Health Council of Hong

Kong conducted a study in the construction industry in 2001 and found that senior management had a positive attitude toward safety culture; supervisors showed fewer positive responses than senior managers; and frontline workers demonstrated the lowest attitude toward safety culture. This study suggested cultivating a strong safety culture in the construction industry, as this industry is one of the most hazardous industries in Hong Kong.

Supervisors also play an important role in ensuring safety in the workplace as well as reminding employees to conform to safety rules and procedures when they perceived that the action of their supervisor was fair (Yule, Flin, and Murdy 2007). On the contrary, they noted from previous surveys that supervisors who demanded more work from their workers demonstrated negative influence on safety climate and supervisors who delegated task-motivated employees to acknowledge their safety accountability.

Cheyne, Oliver, Tomas, and Cox (2002) conducted a study on employee attitudes toward safety in the manufacturing sector in the United Kingdom. The study identified safety standards and goals and safety management, which include personal involvement, communication, workplace hazards, and physical work environment as factors that enhance safety activities in an organization. The study found that a good physical working environment and employee involvement were key factors that contributed to safety activities in organizations.

Safety training and safety policy are also essential determinants to enhance safety performance. *Safety training* is defined as, "knowledge of safety given to employees in order for them to work safely and with no danger to their well being" (Law, Chan, and Pun 2006). Lin and Mills (2001) found that clear policy statements and safety training played an important role in reducing accident rates. Earlier studies discovered the link between safety training and increased safety performance (Huang et al. 2006).

Consequently, effective training assists workers to have a sense of belonging, and thus, is more accountable for safety in their workplace. In addition, a company objective and communication of the objective to all workers is the crucial aspect of effective health and safety management, as lack of communication may hinder employee involvement (Vassie and Lucas 2001).

Even previous researches have shown that high rates of injury and accidents are due to unsatisfactory, or nonexistent, health and safety systems (Lin and Mills 2001). Vassie and Lucas (2001) investigated health and safety management in the manufacturing sectors, and the results indicated that empowered workers who played active health and safety roles could result in health and safety performance improvements, although the empowerment was limited. Although employee participation and involvement are crucial, the accountability and responsibility in the safety and health industry must come from senior management as required by the occupational health and safety legislation (Vassie and Lucas 2001).

In conclusion, many previous studies have shown and debated various dimensions in safety climate, safety culture, and OHS management scale. As such, a combination of different dimensions in an instrument can ensure a high reliability of the health and safety management measurement, and thus, organizations can enhance their understanding of employees' perceptions to ensure improvement of their safety performance.

2.3   OSH Legal Framework in Malaysia

In the early state of country development, the economic structure depended heavily on agricultural- and mining-based activities. The growth of these sectors introduced various hazards to workers such as physical, chemical, radiation, biological, ergonomics and psycho-social. The Selangor Boiler Enactment in 1892 was the first legislation to address industrial safety issues. In 1913, the Machinery Ordinance was enacted to ensure safety of machinery, including boiler and internal combustion engines. The Machinery Ordinance of 1913 was updated in 1932 (Machinery Enactment of 1932) with additional provisions on registration and inspection of machinery installation. The Machinery Ordinance of 1953 superseded all previous legislation related to industrial safety and was enforced in all eleven states of Malaya under the jurisdiction of Machinery Department, Ministry of Labor. Early OSH legislation, the Federated Malay States Mining Enactment of 1926, and the Rump Labor Code of 1933 included public health provisions. Both these legislations required the provision of accommodation, sanitation, medical care and services, decent working conditions, and livable wages for the mine and estate workers.

2.4   Occupational Safety & Health Act 1994

The introduction of a comprehensive Occupational Safety and Health Act (OSHA) 1994 was in response to the need to cover a wider employee base and newer hazards introduced in the workplace. Developed countries such as Japan had enacted such legislation in 1972; United Kingdom in 1974 (the Health and Safety At Work Act 1974); United States of America in 1970 (the Occupational Health & Safety Act 1970; and in Sweden and Norway, the act was called Internal Control Regulation. The OSHA 1994 is enforced by the Department of Occupational Safety and Health (DOSH) under the Ministry of Human Resources. DOSH was previously known as Factory and Machinery Department. The name was changed to reflect changes in coverage.

The act was derived from the philosophy of the Robens Commission and Health & Safety at Work Act 1974 in the United Kingdom, emphasizing self-regulation and duties of employer, employee, and designer and manufacturer. The employer's duties included the provision of a safe system of work, training, maintenance of work environment, and arrangement for minimizing the risks as low as reasonably practicable. In short, the responsibility on OSH is made to rest on those who create the risks (employers) and those who work with the risks (employees).

The act is referred as a reflexive-type of act, which was less prescriptive, to cover all workers except those in armed forces and those who work aboard ships (which were covered by other legislations). The act also emphasized duties of care by individuals, thus empowering the participation of all persons in OSH. Under the OSH Act 1994, National Council for Occupational Safety and Health was established. This council comprised of fifteen council members with tripartite representation from the government, employers, employees, and OSH professionals (with at least one female member). The legislation also contains provision for formulating regulations and Code of Practices (COP), which indicates what should be done, and thus assist the employer to comply with the act.

A series of regulations have been introduced under OSHA 1994. The emphasis of these regulations has been toward establishing mechanism to implement OSH in workplaces. Workplaces with five or more workers are required to formulate a Safety and Health Policy. The Safety and Health Committee Regulations 1996 requires establishments with forty workers and above to establish a safety and health committee. The committee is required to meet at least once in every three months, with the functions to identify hazards at the workplace, institute control measures, investigate incidents, and conduct audits.

In terms of representation in the committee, workplace with fewer than one hundred workers will need to have at least two representatives each for workers and management, respectively. However, workplaces with more than one hundred workers will need to have a minimum of four representatives each for workers and management. The Safety and Health Officer Regulations provide for specific industries to have a Safety and Health Officer (SHO). An SHO is an individual who has attended training in the National Institute of Occupational Safety and Health (NIOSH) or other accredited training bodies and has passed the examination conducted by NIOSH and registered with DOSH.

The Control of Industrial Major Accident Hazards (CIMAH) Regulations 1996 was enacted in response indirectly to the Bhopal disaster in India in 1984 and the Sungai Buloh firecracker factory tragedy in Malaysia, which killed twenty-three workers in 1992.

The Classification, Packaging and Safety Data Sheet for Hazardous Chemical Regulations 2013 and Use and Standard of Exposure of Chemical Hazardous to Health (USECHH) Regulations 2000 were specific for controlling chemicals at the workplace. The CPL regulation required proper packaging and labeling of chemicals by the supplier, including the label giving risk phrases. The USECHH regulation includes the provision of chemical health risk assessor (CHRA), occupational health doctor (OHD), and industrial hygiene technician to perform their respective roles in assessing the health risk from chemical exposure. In particular, the chemical health-risk assessment includes having a list of all chemicals, assessing workers' exposure to these risks, deciding on acceptability of risks and control measures that exist. If risks are found to be unacceptable, action needs to be taken. This regulation leads to increased training needs, which was offered by NIOSH. Guidelines on Chemical Health Risk Assessment have also been issued.

2.5 Implication of ILO Convention & Recommendation on Malaysia Legislation

Malaysia has been the member of the ILO since 1957. To date, Malaysia has ratified fifteen ILO fundamental conventions, and fourteen are in force. Table 7 shows the fundamental ILO conventions that have been ratified by Malaysia as of December 7, 2002. ILO convention and recommendation related to OSH can be classified into four categories: (1) guiding policies for action; (2) protection in given branches of economic activity (e.g., construction industry, commerce, offices, and dock work); (3) protection against specific risks (e.g., ionizing radiation, benzene, asbestos, guarding of machinery); and (4) measures of protection (e.g., medical examinations of young workers, maximum weight of loads to be transported by a single worker, prevention of occupational accidents on board ship, prevention of occupational cancer, and prevention of air pollution, noise, and vibration in the working environment).

An ILO convention is considered a multilateral international treaty and contains binding obligations. Member countries on ratifying a convention are obliged to apply its provision by legislation or by other appropriate means as indicated in the text of the convention. Reports on noncompliance may be made by the governments of other ratifying states or by employers' or workers' organizations. Procedures exist for investigating and acting upon such complaints. Usually, trade unions use ILO standards to support arguments in bargaining and promoting legislation. In the other hands, ILO recommendations are a form of guidelines for action to be taken by member countries that do not require reporting to ILO. The reason why Malaysia has not ratified other ILO OSH conventions is not clearly known; further study is required.

However, on a positive note, Malaysia is keeping pace in OSH development and supporting ILO initiative at the local level. Local regulations, such as Asbestos Regulations, are modeled against the ILO Asbestos Convention 1986. ILO OHS Services Convention 1985 has been referred in the development of the OSH Act 1994. In many instances, local legislation was developed with the adequate advice from ILO experts through various platform and initiatives. In the case of developing the Malaysia OSH-MS, which was undertaken by the National Council of Occupational Safety and Health (NCOSH) in 2001, ILO OSH 2001 was used as the framework to the develop local standard, and an ILO expert was invited to brief the local OSH community. The Malaysia OSH-MS is scheduled to be ready by mid-2003.

Malaysia also participated in the International Program for the Improvement of Working Conditions and Environment (PIACT) organized by ILO in 1993 in line with the initiative under the Chemical Convention 1990 (No. 170) and Recommendation 1990 (No. 177). As part of this exercise, a training module on "Safety and Health in the Use of Chemicals at Work" was published locally (ILO 1991; 1993).

ILO-Japan Institute for Science and Labor (ISC) initiative, such as the Workplace Improvement for Small Enterprise (WISE) project in 1997, was another case where collaboration between local authority and an ILO regional office was carried out. This project was specifically targeted to improve OSH in the small- and medium-sized industries in Malaysia by using low-cost improvement methods. This project was viewed successful at its own right. The follow-up study was carried out among the ex-WISE project participating companies in 2001, and the result showed that the ex-WISE companies had demonstrated some form of OSH management systems, such as OSH committee (Ng et al. 2002). World Bank has also funded the capacity building project for Department of Occupational Safety and Health (DOSH) with the ILO as the advisor.

2.6 Implementation of OSHA 1994

A survey carried out by Idris Md. Yusof (2008) showed that

- 61 percent of the organizations have OSH policies;
- 83 percent of workplaces have safety and health committees;
- 86 percent of major installation have health and safety management systems;
- 38 percent of non-major installations have health and safety management systems; and
- 71 percent of Chemical Industry Council (CICM) members have responsible-care programs.

Since the introduction of Safety Induction for Construction Workers (SICW) was implemented in 1999, there were 240,000 green cardholders up to 2001.

There has also been an increasing number of OSH-competent persons, as required by OSHA 1994. As of 2001, there are about 1,200 Safety and Health Officers (SHO), 30 noise-competent persons, 81 chemical health-risk assessors, and 124 occupational health doctors. The number of OSH practitioners will increase in the coming years. DOSH has also increased the frequency of inspection under the Inspection and Audit Program for the small- and medium-sized industries from 2002 until 2006. Each year, there will be about 2,500 to 3,400 small- and medium-sized industries scheduled to be inspected (Idris Md. Yusof, 2008). This is due to the fact that around 90 percent of the private business establishments in Malaysia are from the small- and medium-sized industries.

Institutions providing various OSH services could be the driving force to enhance the implementation of OSHA 1994. These institutions are as follows:

- DOSH
- SOCSO
- Workers and Environmental Health Unit
- Ministry of Health
- NIOSH
- Local Universities such as UTM, OUM, UNISEL etc.
- Society of Occupational and Environmental Medicine
- Malaysia Medical Association (MMA)
- Malaysian Society for Occupational Safety and Health (MSOSH)
- Malaysian Occupational Health Nurses Association (MOHNA)
- OSH Department in Malaysian Trades Union Congress (MTUC)
- Various consumer and environmental groups, such as Sahabat Alam Malaysia (SAM) and Consumers' Association of Penang (CAP)

2.7 Safety Policy and Culture

The safety legislation and policies have a great impact upon the safety level of a workplace. The safety policy is actually the guiding principle of organization, which is a statement from top management that declares their commitment to the statements in the policy. The safety policy statement is a document that sets out the organization that will manage safety in the workplace. Employees can use the statement to guide their action in handling their task. The policy statement is very important, because the law requires it. All the organizations with more than four employees have to develop this policy. Under OSHA Act section 16: Duty to formulate safety and health policy. This clause mentioned that "the duty of every employer and every self-employed person is to prepare and as often as may be appropriate revise a written statement of his general policy with respect to the safety and health at work of his employees and the organization and arrangements for the time being in force for carrying out that policy, and to bring the statement and any revision of it to the notice of all of his employees."

A safety culture should be established in an organization and at the workplace. Strong support and encouragement from all levels from top management to the ordinary worker are needed. With the support of the management, the culture of safety will be established, and this will increase enthusiasm and motivation in the employee to think and work safely. There are duties for everyone to promote safety, because it will bring many benefits to the organization. Some other benefits include

- enhancing awareness for occupational safety and health policy;
- informing employees that organization management are responsible of employees
- informing employees that they have a role to play for everyone's good;
- increasing morale of workers; and
- increasing productivity for the organization.

One way to make the safety culture more visible is through the use of employee perception surveys, which have been valuable tools for detecting differences in employee attitudes concerning several management practices. Ojanen et al. (1988) suggested that safety performance should be measured on multiple levels, one of them being safety attitudes, in order to determine the real safety level of an organization. They claimed that measuring safety climate can indicate changes in organizational safety practices and would therefore be useful for evaluating safety programs and suggested that a safety climate questionnaire is the only way to measure safety climate in an organization.

2.8 Management of Safety and Performance

The top management is accountable and responsible to provide all the relevant resources to ensure excellent safety performance. A study by Mearns (et al. 2003) stated that safety management practices exhibit the safety culture of top management, while safety climate was considered as the specific indicator of overall safety culture. As a result, good safety management practices were revealed in improved safety climate of the entire team. *Safety management practices* refer to the important practices, accountability, and performance related to safety. Management needs to address positive values and intentions toward safety; hence employees understand safety and make decision on safety as their main concern. Mearns et al. (2003) found that several safety climate scales to be linked to statistics of official accident and also the number of respondents reporting accident. In conclusion, overall scores of safety management practices were associated with reduced accidents rates.

Mearns et al. (2003), showed that occupational safety at the organizational level was positively related to a high-performance work system. Additional study by Mearns (et al. 2003) was on safety performance, which measured in two terms. The first term was personal safety orientation inclusive of safety knowledge, safety motivation, safety compliance, and safety initiative. Trust in management and perceived safety climate mediated the relationship between the high-performance work systems and safety outcome. Employees' perceptions on management safety intention were essential. Study findings by Gyekye and Salminen (2007) revealed that employees who have good perceptions on their organization will also have high job satisfaction and tend to be more compliant to the organization safety management policies. Six management practices inclusive of management commitment, rewards, communication and feedback, selection, training, and participation were tested, which are normal factors in safety programs. After performing a factor analysis, six factor scales were developed from the management practices scale, which reliably predicted injury rates. Hence, Gyekye and Salminen suggested that the most effective steps to be look into were hiring safety-conscious personnel during the recruitment process and giving them appropriate occupational safety training.

2.9   Safety Practices and Performance

A study by Zohar (1980) highlighted that the most important aspect to verify success of safety programs in any organization were management commitment toward safety with consistence of multiple factors, such as establishment of job-training programs, executive authorization to safety administrators, involvement of high-level managers in safety committees, and safety in job design that includes workplace necessity. Management should not view safety as a separate function of technical and independent job processes; instead, it should be equally valued within the overall management operation's functions. Zohar's study disclosed that there were two climate levels that have highly influenced determining safety climate levels, namely (1) the importance of training to sustain successful performance and (2) followed by required working experience in safety requirement for the related work activities.

Hayes (et al. 1998) supported the study findings conducted by Zohar (1980), as they confirmed that WSS subscales recorded significant relation to the frequency of safety awareness training and whether or not employees received a safety orientation when entering their jobs. This group of employees who received safety orientation reported to have safer perceptions on work environment compared to employees who were not receiving a safety orientation. Furthermore, O'Toole (2002) stated that "to make the value's principle on safety and health subject that is so called safety culture more observable, a perception survey of employees was recommended." The WSS also applied to measure several safety programs' effectiveness.

Finally, according to Huang (et al. 2006), organizational factors contributed to workplace safety had been centered to decrease injuries in the workplace. They reminded, as safety training given by management does not carry meaning and prove that management was fully concerned on safety, this could influenced the employees' rating given to training as excellent because of lack of other safety related efforts. Overall, the factorial evidence verified the entire mediated predictors were important dimensions of a safety climate. Significant relationship in positive direction was found within safety variable however in negative direction with injury incidence. The data proved that the relationship between safety climate and occupational injury were mediated by employee safety control, and the history of self-reported injury was predicted by safety climate as a dominant factor.

2.10 Lifesaving Rules

These lifesaving rules are clear and simple dos and don'ts covering activities with the highest-potential safety risk. The lifesaving rules do not replace or invalidate the golden rules (comply, intervene, and respect) or any other business, operation, or safety rules in force, especially in the oil and gas industry, such as Brooke Dockyard.

The twelve lifesaving rules are as follows:

1. Work with a valid work permit when required.
2. Conduct gas tests when required.
3. Verify isolation before work begins and use the specified life-protecting equipment.

4. Obtain authorization before entering a confined space.
5. Obtain authorization before overriding or disabling safety critical equipment.
6. Protect yourself against a fall when working at height.
7. Do not walk under a suspended load.
8. Do not smoke outside of designated smoking areas.
9. No alcohol or drugs while working or driving.
10. While driving, do not use your phone, and do not exceed speed limits.
11. Wear your seat belt when driving or riding in a car.
12. Follow prescribed Journey Management Plan.

These twelve lifesaving rules applied in Shell and their subsidiary. The appointed contractors required to adopt and apply these twelve lifesaving rules into their assigned project. By reviewing the twelve lifesaving rules with an immediate supervisor allows employees to know the purpose and application of each rule and the consequences for non-compliance. The safety supervisor is required to report all non-compliance or potential violations of the lifesaving rules to the officer in charge immediately. It is encourage and support worksite peer-to-peer intervention and observation processes.

2.10.1 Lifesaving Rules Toolbox Talk Guide

A Toolbox Talk is a prejob safety meeting with the whole crew associated with a defined task and is conducted at the worksite discussing the JHA/JSA, which includes understanding the job steps, hazards, threats, control, recovery, roles, and responsibilities. Toolbox meetings are necessary to maintain a high level of safety awareness on the worksite. The meetings are also very useful to encourage the workforce to actively take part in worksite accident prevention. Supervisors are to promote a high level of safety awareness by their example, behavior, and encouragement. At toolbox meetings, employees are informed of the workforce in their charge on the nature of the hazard and the risks identified by the assessments, the preventative and protective measures, emergency procedures, and the relevant competent personnel.

Supervisor shall ensure the following at the construction site:

- Tool Box talks are scheduled daily at worksite each day;
- talks are held during normal working hours with provisions of fifteen to twenty minutes downtime at the discretion of the supervisor;
- all the operative-level workforces will attend their respective supervisor's Toolbox Talks;
- permit applicant/worksite supervisor will brief the crew at the Toolbox Talk;
- the number of workers should not be too large. It is recommended that workers should be separated in groups of ten to twenty workers per Toolbox Talk;
- the Toolbox Talks should focus on accident prevention and not as a forum to air personal grievances; and
- the Toolbox Talks are presented in the language and understanding of the operators and workers.

The Toolbox Talks are to encourage two-way communication on work and safety matters and should not be restricted to the reading out of a list of dos and don'ts. Subjects for discussion should be chosen based on what activities are being carried out (e.g., working at heights, confine space entry, hot work involving welding). As required, the safety department is to support the presenter whom will provide subject material. The subject material should vary at each presentation and not be unnecessarily repetitive. Each Toolbox Talk is to be recorded by the supervisor on a Toolbox Record Sheet. The Toolbox Talks are to be closely monitored by the project management and safety supervisors. Toolbox Talks (about relevant issues—suitable and sufficient) have an emphasis on safety by the supervisor. The main goal is to ensure nobody gets hurt during the course of the work being carried out and to ensure improvement of safety culture.

2.10.2   Policy

It is a corporation requirement that every employee actively participate in the Toolbox Talk and any scheduled or unscheduled safety meetings. The purpose is the element established the minimum OSH Management System responsibilities for the performance of Toolbox Talk.

2.10.3   Responsibilities

i. Employees

It is recognized that the employees and their participation in the Toolbox Talk is a key to the success of the overall HSE program. Although the reason for some of the OSH policies and procedures may not be at first apparent to the worker, it is felt that worker understanding and communication can be achieved through worker training and these meetings.

ii. Supervision

It shall be the responsibility of each member of the supervision to ensure that the OSH procedures set forth in the HSE manual and any client requirements are discussed during Toolbox Talk. In addition, it shall be their responsibility to ensure safe work practices are discussed and prejob planning techniques, such as JHA and JSA are discussed and planned for.

iii. Line Management

The line management must assure the implementation of the use of Toolbox Talk at each facility or location, in addition to accepting total responsibility for implementation of the policies and procedures set forth in the HSE manual.

a. Line managers shall familiarize themselves with this element in order to ensure adequate site implementation procedures are in place.

b. Line managers may, if the need arises, implement site-specific procedures more stringent to provide an even safer workplace according to the need.

c. It shall additionally be the responsibility of the line manager to ensure that a positive HSE philosophy is communicated to the employees during these meetings.

iv. HSE Manager

The HSE manager will assist executive management in developing and maintaining a basic Toolbox Talk program. The HSE manager will work with line management and supervisors to implement and maintain an effective Toolbox Talk system. Weekly reports summarizing HSE activities, including the maintenance of these meetings throughout the corporation, will be submitted to executive management. It should be noted that the executive management of the corporation advocates a strong incident prevention program. Executive management fully endorses and requires that daily Toolbox Talks are performed. One benefit is that these meetings help prevent human suffering and individual hardships to our employees and directly contributes to improvement of morale, which, in turn, results in better productivity and quality.

2.11   Permit to Work (PTW)

Permit to work (PTW) is a job authorization process that includes a systematic approach to identifying task-specific hazards and associated controls, individual responsibilities, and communication to affected personnel. Organizations or companies are expected to have and adhere to a permitting system.

Mandatory requirements for all fabrication personnel include the following:

a. Ensure that a location list of jobs that require a permit are posted on a display board available for all workers.

b. Verify that a location-specific list of jobs requiring a permit is discussed during site-specific orientations and that an appropriate filing system is properly maintained and coordinated.

c. For all issued permits, ensure that adequate planning and time are allowed for effective development, review, issue, execution, and closure of work permits.

d. Review and concur with all contractor-issued permits before work begins.

e. As a minimum, permits must contain the following:
- location where work will be performed
- contractor performing the work
- supervisor (with company name) responsible for the work group
- description for the work to be performed
- prerequisites for the work
- concurrence and approval for work to start
- all permits shall have attached Job Safety Analysis (JSA)
- prejob walk-through prior to the permitted work
- actions to ensure the permits are properly closed out
- verify that permitted activities are conducted as written
- inform the supervisor of contractors who do not have or use their PTW process

2.11.1 Purpose

The permit to work (PTW) system procedure is a management tool to ensure the safety of those doing the work and that of others. It also ensures that the overall health, safety, and environmental aspect and the integrity of the installation and its surrounding workplace is not put at risk. This procedure complies with OSHA 94, Section 15, subsection 2(a) and HSE requirement on ensuring the health and safety of all persons and of safeguarding the natural environment.

A PTW system is a formal written system used to control work that is identified as potentially dangerous. It is also a means of communication between site management, supervisors, and operators and those who carry out the work. The system aims to ensure that proper planning and precautions are given to the hazards and risks of a particular job. The permit is a written document that authorizes certain people to carry out specific work at a certain time and place, and it sets out the main precautions needed to complete the work safely.

The terms *PTW*, *permit*, or *work permit* refer to the certificate or form that is used as part of an overall system of work management that has been devised by the corporation to meet its specific needs. A PTW system is an important part of the HSE management system because of its control over hazards and managing risks at the worksite. The understanding of PTW is therefore essential for all worksite supervisors to ensure that proper authorization is given before OSH-critical work is performed.

The procedure thus falls within the elements of the Hazards and Effects Management process in the corporation's HSE-MS. A critical element of the PTW preparation stage is an assessment of the hazards, threats, and risk, which are associated with the work to be undertaken. The techniques of the Hazard and Effect Management Process (HEMP) is to be applied to help the assessor:

a. Identify: Understand the hazards and threats associated with the work: What are the impacts to people, environment, or assets? Obtain precise details of the work to be undertaken. Are there process hazards associated with the material being handled in the work?

b. Assess: Recognize the risks: What is the likelihood of harmful instances occurring? Is the risk involved as low as reasonably practicable (ALARP)? Consider the practical difficulties of carrying out the work; if necessary. consulting the discipline specialists undertaking the work.

c. Control: Decide upon the barriers and control necessary to manage the risk, thus providing a safe working environment: What is required to prevent the likelihood of causing harm from carrying out the work being realized? Are there any safer alternatives either in terms of timing or the intended method of performance of the work?

d. Recover: Agree on the recovery measures in the event that controls break down.

The permit applicant should carry out such assessments in conjunction with his workforce and any other persons whose specialist knowledge may be needed. Where available, the permit applicant will take advantage of all hazard information in part 2 of the HSE Case. This will assist him in recognizing major accidents' hazards, threats, risks, barriers, and precautions needed and using a response mechanism, should controls break down. Likewise, the permit authorizer and the work approver should also undertake such assessments when the permit is presented to further enhance safety control, if needed.

2.11.2   Target Audience

This procedure is to be used by all staff and contractors who work in BIF. Other requirements will be as per the Bridging Document and Site Specific Procedure for the particular activity.

2.11.3   Scope

This procedure describes the requirements of the PTW System in line with the "Principles of Permitry" in the execution of all work where OSH is a constraint, in Brooke Dockyard operations. It is a safety critical procedure and is one of the key management systems to ensure that proper planning and consideration are given to the risks arising from the hazards of a particular job and that the precautions needed are set out to complete the job safely.

The requirements include the application of the "Principles of Permitry," which shall be adopted in deciding the application of the PTW system and the responsibilities, training, competency, and method in terms of preparation, process, and completion and use of the PTW Application Form during implementation.

2.12 Training Program

Training is widely understood as, "communication directed at a defined population for the purpose of developing skills, modifying behavior, and increasing competence." Generally, training focuses exclusively on *what* needs to be known. Whereas, *education* is a longer-term process that incorporates the goals of training and explains *why* certain information must be known. Education emphasizes the scientific foundation of the material presented.

Both training and education induce learning, a process that modifies knowledge and behavior through teaching and experience. The research model described here pertains to both training and education. Therefore, in this document, *training* refers to both processes. In contrast to informal training (which is embedded in most instances of human exchange), formal training interventions have stated goals, content, and strategies for instruction. Our intent is to offer a general approach to intervention effectiveness research that addresses formal training across settings and topics. The model integrates primary and secondary data collection with qualitative and quantitative analyses so that the benefits of each research technique can be applied to the evaluation of training effectiveness.

Training intervention effectiveness research is needed to (1) identify major variables that influence the learning process and (2) optimize resources available for training interventions. Logical and progressive study models are best suited to identify the critical elements and causal relationships that affect training effectiveness and efficiency. In training research, it is often difficult to arrive at definitive answers. Therefore, if training is to be an essential component of planned interventions, a uniform system of research is needed to explain how training is made effective and to indicate how resources for training should be organized.

2.12.1   Trainee Reactions (Level 1)

Trainee reaction, the first level of the Four-Level Evaluation Model, is a measure of a trainee's feelings about a training program as described by Tan (et al. 2003). It is the most common criterion used in the industry to evaluate training programs as reported by Saari (et al. 1988). However, the arguments are continuously going on, and researchers have consistently questioned the overusage of trainee reaction as a sole predictor for determining the effectiveness of a training program—for example, by Ruona (et al. 2002) and Tan (et al. 2003). Noe and Schmitt (1986) have suggested that trainee satisfaction has no significant relationship with learning.

Similarly, Warr and Bunce (1995) found no significant correlation between reported enjoyment of training, usefulness of training, and learning scores. However, there is a strong correlation between a learning score and job performance. Alliger (et al. 1997) identified one effort to overcome this problem was to evaluate trainee reactions and feedback on effectiveness of the training program. Other studies conducted by Morgan and Casper (2000) and Tan (et al. 2003) had further emphasized the importance of understanding the multidimensional nature of trainee reactions. In their meta analyses, Alliger (et al. 1997) showed that stronger correlations were found between utility reactions and learning or job performance than between affective reaction measures and learning or job performance.

Hence, Ruona (et al. 2002) concluded that the relationship between utility reactions and the predictors of learning transfer. They suggested utility reactions for learning outcome evaluations, rather than traditional affective reactions.

2.12.2. Learning (Level 2)

Learning, which is level 2 of the Four-Level Evaluation Model, is defined as "principles, facts, and techniques understood and absorbed by the trainees" Alliger and Janak (1989). As mentioned earlier, many researchers have argued the need for more detailed evaluation for learning outcomes to better present the multifaceted nature of learning. To fulfill these needs, many researchers in the field of education, industrial organizational psychology, and training have developed a number of frameworks.

For example, Gagne (1984) categorized learning outcomes into intellectual skills (procedural knowledge), verbal information (declarative knowledge), cognitive strategies (executive control process), motor skills, and attitudes. This classification strengthened instructional objectives, enabling them to examine not only the behavioral domain but also various cognitive, skill-oriented, and attitudinal learning outcomes (Gagne 1984).

In addition, Kraiger (et al. 1993) proposed categories of learning outcomes that involved Cognitive Outcomes, Skill-Based Outcomes and Affective Outcomes; they then explained each category with recommendations for evaluation measurements. This was supported by Alliger (et al. 1997) in their meta-analysis classified learning (level 2) into three categories: immediate knowledge, knowledge retention, and behavior/skill demonstration. The first category, immediate knowledge, utilizes multiple-choice test responses, open-ended questions, and listing of facts to evaluate trainees' knowledge. The second category, knowledge retention, is similar to immediate knowledge but administered at a later point of time rather than just after training. The last category, behavior/skill demonstration, comprises any indicators of behavioral proficiency that are measured during the training.

2.12.3 Skill Acquisition

Rosenbaum and Carlson (2001) elaborated that *skill* was "an ability that allows a goal to be achieved within some domain with increasing likelihood as a result of practice." In this regard, *skill acquisition* can be considered as, "attaining capabilities by practice, which helps increase the possibility of goal achievement." Many researchers have broken down skill acquisition into various phases for better understanding. For example, Snoddy (1926) introduced two stages, adaptation and facilitation, to explain the learning curve. In the adaptation stage, the improvement depends on more than repetition, while the facilitation stage depends on repetition alone. Fitts (1964) subsequently suggested three stages of skill acquisition. In the first stage, or cognitive stage, a considerable amount of cognitive activity is required to encode the skill into a form that will make it possible for learners to generate the desired behavior. The primary goal for the learners in this stage is to know what is to be done rather than to improve their motor patterns. Therefore, improvements can be observed through verbal mediation. The second stage of skill acquisition, the associative stage, involves a gradual improvement on performance.

Errors can be detected and eliminated by practice so that the performance level becomes more consistent. Further, verbal mediation reduces, and the learner focuses more on "how to do" rather than "what to do." In Fitts's study (1964), the last phase, the autonomous stage, learners can automatically perform the required skill. The performance requires less mental workload, and secondary tasks can be performed with less interference.

Furthermore, Anderson (1982) offered a broader explanation of Fitts's three stages but used a different lexicon. In his construction, the declarative stage, the knowledge compilation, and the procedural stage, respectively, correspond to Fitts's three stages of skill acquisition. However, while utilizing similar underlying concepts, Anderson emphasized the knowledge type in each stage. For example, he notes that the declarative stage mostly utilizes verbal mediation, and the procedural stage focuses on performance itself. The knowledge compilation is a conversion phase from the declarative to procedural stage.

In the lifting and lowering training program, factual and conceptual information is provided to support trainees' understanding of knowledge and skills. However, the training program gradually emphasizes the trainees' performance more, since the ultimate goal focuses more on the level of performance.

The first hypothesis of this study, that learning outcomes regarding application will be more predictive of training performance, can be supported by Fitts's and Anderson's three stages of skill acquirement. It can be expected that predictors that involve the actual application of performance will more accurately anticipate training performance than will those who rely upon factual or conceptual knowledge. Additionally, it is likely that multidimension of knowledge and cognitive abilities are involved throughout skill acquisition. This supports the multidimension of learning outcomes related to the lifting and lowering training program, which is reviewed in the following paragraphs.

2.12.4   Multidimension of Learning Outcomes

Goldstein and Ford (2002) defined *training* as "the systematic acquisition of skills, rules, concepts, or attitudes that result in improved performance in another environment." It is a specialized form of education that focuses on developing or improving performance. Rekus (1999) argued that an education, on the other hand, focuses on whether learners have gained knowledge and skills but does not evaluate actual performance or application in a different environment. That is, simply understanding and knowing a specific subject does not warrant an effective training system. An effective training system must ensure that learners are able to perform the expected outcomes in such a way that they have demonstrably learned during the training.

Researchers have become more aware of the significance of the multidimensional nature of learning, such as Bloom (1956), Gagne (1984), and Krathwohl (et al. 1964), and have tried to apply those theories in designing and evaluating training systems by Kraiger (et al. 1993).

2.12.5 Roles Providing Safety Training

i. *Safety Training Program*

The existence of a safety training program is important for a safe working practice. It is the integration of a safe working practice by teaching workers the facts about accident causes and indicating the preventive measures to be taken. Equally important, however, is the requirement of further training programs for the skilled supervisor or worker, whose techniques may need bringing up-to-date and into whose earlier training accident prevention may not have been integrated to the extent now realized to be essential (Petersen 1984).

ii. *Exposure to Safety Training*

Exposure to safety training is a development of a safety training program for all employees potentially exposed to safety during hazardous maintenance operations, and they must receive training on how to respond to expected emergencies. Maintenance employees must not performed any operation unless trained to the level required by the job function and responsibility. They must also be certified by a qualified instructor, as having completed training (Grimaldi 1989)

iii. *Alert Workers and Teach Skills and Knowledge of Safety Practices*

Training alerts workers to potential hazards they may encounter and teaches knowledge and skills needed to perform work with minimal risk (Nicole 1988).

iv. *Conducting a Safety Orientation Program*

Conducting a safety orientation program is the initial step toward safety training. It is needed for new employees who are likely to be exposed to risk before their job training is completed.

It should familiarize new employees with common types of hazards and the precautions that they are expected to take. It should also cover the board requirements of contractors' own accident prevention policy (e.g., if it is company policy that safety helmets and protective footwear should always be worn, then they should be made clear and should be told how and where to obtain them) (Grimaldi 1989).

v. The Use of Persuasion

The training providing safety skills and information should be supplemented by the techniques of persuasion. Persuasion has an important function. Its most common form is a postal used to indicate bad habits, pinpoint the advantages of safer working habits, or give detailed information, advice, or instruction on special points.

2.13 Behavior Change

The discussion of behavioral change has focused particularly on the insights that behavioral theory and empirical research can add to the fundamental building block of behavioral change for policy makers—the rational choice model. These additional insights are especially useful when dealing with psychologically complex behaviors. The traditional policy tools that flow from the rational choice model will, however, generally still form a core part of a comprehensive approach to achieving widespread, sustainable behavioral change. Action needs to be taken on a range of fronts within an integrated, longer-term strategy for maximum behavioral change. The different policy tools used by government that potentially influence a certain public behavior should be internally consistent and mutually supportive within this integrated strategy.

Safety assessment is a process used to determine a contractor's compliance with or ability to meet specific safety rules and requirements set by the government safety regulations or by safety and environmental organizations. Safety rules or criteria are needed to accomplish the work with high overall performance. Any deviation from these safety requirements will affect the contractor's overall performance.

Safe acts and safe conditions in performing maintenance and construction works have been receiving wide attention in the safety engineering and management literature. Duff (et al. 1994) conducted a study in the development and effects of behaviorally based management techniques in improving site safety. Goal-setting and feedback methods were developed and tested on sites. Measures of safety performance were taken before, during, and after the application of these methods. The result shows that safety behavior can be objectively and reliably measured, without excessive use of managerial or supervisory resources, producing performance data that can be used in many different safety management strategies, which will produce large improvements in safety performance. Also, it shows that the commitment of the site management appears to enhance the effectiveness of the goal-setting and feedback approach. J. Giustina and D. Giustina (1989) conducted a research study on quality of work life through employee motivation. The findings of this study illustrated three important contributions management can offer employees to improve safety in the workplace:

i. Knowledge and understanding of safe and healthy work practices: employees must be trained to identify present and potential hazards not only in the jobs they are performing but in jobs being performed nearby.

ii. A strongly shared belief that top management is truly committed to safety and health: workers must know that top management is willing to devote resources to improve safety and health in the workplace.

iii. Management's recognition and support for changes in work behavior to achieve the desired safe work behaviors will stimulate workers to take responsibility for change.

Heinrich (et al. 1980) has studied the contribution of both unsafe acts and unsafe conditions. He analyzed 75,000 accidents and found that 88 percent were caused by unsafe acts or unsafe operation; 10 percent from unsafe conditions or unsafe work locations; and 2 percent from unpreventable causes (Baruer 1990). Hinze, Bern, and Piepho (1995) conducted a study of the importance of Experience Modification Rating (EMR) as a measure of safety performance. This rating is used to adjust the cost of workers' compensation insurance premiums. This modifier is essentially an incentive for firms to strive for good safety records, as firms with poor safety records will pay higher premiums. Results show how a frequency rate has a larger impact on the EMR than does severity rate. The EMR is noticeably reduced when hourly wages paid are increased. It is also reduced when the total wages paid per year are increased. Findings suggested that the EMR is not an appropriate measure of safety performance for all companies.

Jannadi and Assaf (1990) assessed the safety practices in different jobsites in Saudi Arabia with varying project sizes using ???based on number of employees????. They found that the safety level in jobsites varies with the project size. Large projects have a better average safety level than small projects. They concluded that the safety level is mainly related to the nationality and the type of the project. The assessment results showed that there is a need for a safety code in Saudi Arabia, which should be strictly applied to protect workers and property.

Lateiner (1969) conducted a study of the importance of attitude in controlling incidents and improving safety performance. Through a survey for supervisors of forty-seven companies, Lateiner found that as a positive attitude toward safety increased, the number of accidents per employee dramatically decreased. He concluded that the development of a sound safety attitude throughout an enterprise was predicated on how well supervisors met safety responsibilities. Consequently, accidents will decrease when attitudes improve as a result of supervisors effectively performing safety procedures.

McCook (1988) reviewed a study on three groups of Ontario construction contractors, devoting essentially the same resources to safety. One group that had made employees responsible for improved safety had "consistently poor results," according to the study. A second group, which gave supervisors "the responsibility and the accountability to make an effective change in the accident rate," had better-than-average results. Because the supervisors were held accountable, they initiated formal inspections, training programs, accident investigations, and tool checks. The most successful group employed "management techniques of planning, directing, and controlling." The contractors in this group established quality and safety standards for their organizations and developed safe work procedures (Grimaldi 1989).

2.14   Empirical Studies on Safety Performance

There is a significant relationship between safety requirement with safety compliance; for example, compliance with safe working practices and accidents occurred had been common features in literatures related to safety at workplace in various fields of employment. According to Hart (2000), most of the studies had found affirmative relationships between self-reported safety practices and safety climates, where, in turn, both variables were negatively related to accidents frequency. This explained that when non-compliance with safety requirement, it was the result of improper safety management where finally contributed to the incidents. From this perspective, safety climate comprises organizational safety policies and work procedures, which derives from organizational norm principles and expectation, decision-making, and safety principles together with organizational obligation to safety manners (Hahn and Murphy 2008). High commitment shown by an organization on workplace safety measurement would contribute to the positive perceptions regarding safe working environment. Kelloway and Francis (2008) supported the above-mentioned factors and suggested management needed to have apparent and enacted safety policies in place and must be implemented and planned. An employee's perception is of the utmost importance; safety climate has been linked to better adherence to safe work behaviors and few accident-related injuries.

Griffin and Neal (2000) agreed with Meams (et al. 2003), by indicating that safety compliance and safety perceptions are two separate safety behaviors components that differentiated them from safety-related performance. For them, safety compliance is adhering to standard work practices, such as utilizing personal protective equipment, whereas safety participation is defined as supportive behavior in a safety environment.

Hofmann and Morgeson (1999) highlighted that employees tend to reciprocate safety procedures adherence in a safety-concerned workplace. They said that a positive safety climate can be a signal to employees that their supervisors were concerned for their safety and welfare.

From the general review on available literatures, this study will examine safety practices in the workplace by adopting Workplace Safety Scale (WSS) developed by Hayes (et al 1998) and recently tested by Ratnawills Md. Ambia (2010) in her study on "Understanding Employees Compliance with Safety Behavior in a Telecommunication Industry." This model consists of five constructs of predictors' variables, namely job safety, coworker safety, supervisor safety, management safety practices, and perception on safety programs applied by the organization on compliance with safety practices.

2.15   Chapter Summary

In conclusion, this chapter has briefly discussed feedback on the OSH Induction Program, which is one of the OSH training programs implemented by Brooke Dockyard. The literature review sections enhanced knowledge and understanding for this study.

Chapter 3

RESEARCH METHODOLOGY

3.1 Introduction

This chapter describes the research design, population, and sample of the OSH Induction Program, the instrument and procedures used to collect data, and how data is computed and analyzed using specific software. This study employed a questionnaire approach to collect data and analyze using SPSS to generate descriptive and inferential statistic.

3.2 Research Framework

The framework indicates the interconnection of all constructs as independent variables with the dependent variables of the study.

3.3 Research Instruments

The research instrument for this study (shown in appendix 4) to be used is modified from previous questionnaires. The questionnaires are divided into five sections, which describe accordingly as shown in table 3.1.

Table 3.1. Questionnaire's component.

Section	Components
A	Demographic Background
B	Knowledge on OSH Induction Course
C	Perception on Organization Safety Management
D	Safety Program/Policies Adopted by the Organization
E	Perception on Safety Behavior at the Workplace

For section C to E, a five-point Likert scale will be used because it allows accurate assessment of opinions, which are often conceptualized in terms of gradation. This scale is commonly used to measure responses and allows respondents to express the degree of their opinion (Evans and Lindsay 2002). Respondents were required to respond to the statements by using a five-point Likert scale as shown in table 3.2.

Table 3.2: The Likert scale used in the questionnaires.

Code	Strongly Disagree	Disagree	Undecided	Agree	Strongly Agree
Value	1	2	3	4	5

The completed questionnaire will be distributed to the respondents with minimal guidance to ensure that they answered properly. Before data are processed, the questionnaires need to go through data screening and a purification process. Data screening is purposely for validation and verification by removing incomplete responses, treatment of missing values, coding, and entry. Whereas data purification is assessing data reliability and "unidimensionality" statistically and measuring used to test for reliability prior to any further analysis.

3.4 Population and Sampling

Singleton and Straits (2005) noted that an experienced researcher always gets a clear picture of the population before selecting the sample. Sampling is part of the element in the population. While simple in principle, sampling can be fraught with difficulties in practice. However, sampling is an important subject in statistics, and it is easier to ask more questions with a sample. Sampling is economical, convenient, and can provide quicker results, and a good sample must be valid in terms of precision.

In this study, the population consists of 712 employees working at Brooke Dockyard. These groups are selected because they are dealing with high-hazard activities. Sampling techniques in this study will include a random sampling according to quota for each section. This sampling's concept is a random selection, a controlled procedure that assures each population a known nonzero chance of being selected as a sample. Simple random sampling, which is the simplest form of probability sampling, was applied for this study. Zikmund (2003) supported that this sampling type has equal chances to be selected. Hence, this study will try to include about 173 respondents as an ideal representative as shown in table 3.3.

Table 3.3: Population and sample size.

	Population	Sample Size (25%)
Project Management Team (PMT)	50	13
QA/HSE Team	60	15
Yard Fabrication Team	120	30
Structural Fabrication Team	150	38
Scaffolding Team	25	6
Blasting/Painting Team	40	10
Electrical & Instrument Team	43	11
HVAC Team	20	5
Piping Team	40	10
GRE Fabrication Team	35	9

Cranage Operation Team	15	4
Material Coordination Team	20	5
Yard Maintenance Team	14	4
Rigging Team	20	5
Architectural Team	40	10
Total	**692**	**175**

3.5 Pilot Test

Pilot study refers to a trial study that is being administered to a selected small group of respondents using the instrument that is similar to the actual study. This pilot study is meant to test the reliability and the validity of the items in the questionnaire that are to be answered by the respondents in the study (Konting 2005). By using this pilot study, researchers would be able to identify the items that need to be improvised or deleted in order to produce a questionnaire of high degree of reliability and validity. The reliability of the questionnaire can be assured through its Cronbach's Alpha level. Cronbach's Alpha is the reliability coefficient that shows the correlation of all the items to form one set of questions (Sekaran 2005). The closer the alpha is to 1.0, the higher the internal reliability of the item. The alpha value that falls below 0.6 is considered weak, while the alpha value that falls between 0.6 and 0.7 can be accepted. The alpha value that is higher than 0.8 is considered good (Hair et al. 2007). Therefore, the minimum alpha value that has been set for this study is 0.7.

For those purposes, about twenty sets of questionnaires will be distributed to the respondents with duration of period required to accomplish the questionnaire also taken into consideration. From the initial findings, changes and amendments will be done if necessary to synergize the instrument. These respondents were being chosen to represent other employees from the studied organization. They were required to answer the questionnaire with minimal guidance from the researcher. The data obtained from this pilot study will be analyzed using SPSS 18.0 software. After that, the researcher analyzed every component to generate the Cronbach's alpha to determine the internal consistency (Cronbach 1951).

3.6   Data Analysis

The raw data obtained from the questionnaires will be analyzed using the Statistical Package for Social Science (SPSS) Version 18.0 to test the research hypotheses constructed and the objective of the study. The raw data were analyzed using two types of statistics, which are: descriptive and inferential statistics. SPSS was used to get an accurate result that minimized errors (Konting 2005). Besides that, Chua (2006) mentioned without statistics, the collected data is difficult to analyze, explain, and understand.

3.6.1 Descriptive Statistics

According to Barrow (2000), *descriptive statistics* is "a set of statistical procedure that described a set of data with no attempt to generalize the result to any other group." Descriptive statistics help to summarize data collected and provide meaningful information to the researcher. It is to describe the distribution of a single variable (dependent variable) and helps to understand the relationship between the studied variables (independent variables and dependent variable). The descriptive statistics used in this study include: frequencies, percentage, mean, and standard deviation. Each statistic has its own purpose. Frequencies and percentage provide simple nominal level data.

3.6.2 Inferential Statistics

According to Barrow (2000), *inferential statistics* is a "statistical procedure designed to allow researcher to make generalizations or inferences regarding population parameters based an analysis of sample statistics." It allows us to draw conclusions about a population from the sample.

3.6.3   Reliability Analysis

Reliability analysis concerns with the accuracy, precision, and consistency of a measure but not validity, which focuses on questions of what is actually being measured. If the measurement is not reliable, it means valid (Cooper and Schindle 2008). Cronbach's alpha was used as a reliability coefficient that indicates how well the items in a set were positively correlated to one another (Cronbach 1951). In general, coefficient alpha would range from 0.00 to 1.00. A figure below 0.600 would have a Poor Strength in Coefficient; 0.600 to 0.700 would be Moderate Strength in Coefficient; 0.700 to 0.800 would be a Good Strength in Coefficient; and 0.800 to 0.900 would have excellent Strength in Coefficient. The closer Cronbach's alpha to 1.000, the higher the internal consistency reliability (Cronbach 1951). Hence, the reliability analysis was used in this study to ensure the results were valid and research findings were consistent to describe the reliability of measurement.

3.6.4   Correlation Analysis

In this study, statistical analysis in the form of Pearson's correlation coefficient was used to measure the strength of the relationship between independent and dependent variables. The Pearson correlation coefficient was utilized to test the research hypotheses concerning the relationship between variables that determine the relationship between the factors. Pearson correlation value, which has a value between -1 and +1, determines the strength and direction of the relationship between two variables (Cooper and Schinder 2008). The prediction of strength of relationship between variables by Miller (1991) is shown in table 3.4.

Table 3.4: Interpretation of the value of
Pearson Correlation Coefficient.

Correlation coefficient r (+/ -)	Relationship between variables
0.0 – 0.20	Little or no relationship
0.20 – 0.40	Some slight relationship
0.40 – 0.60	Substantial relationship
0.60 – 0.80	Strong useful relationship
0.80 – 1.00	High relationship

Source: Miller (1991)

3.7 Chapter Summary

In this chapter, the research methodology, design and frameworks, subjects, the instrument, how the pilot-test to be carried out, administration of questionnaire, and data analysis were discussed in detail. The analysis of the data and the results will be discussed thoroughly in the following chapter.

Chapter 4

STUDY FINDINGS

4.1 Introduction

This chapter presents the data analysis and the results feedback from 173 sets of questionnaire forms were distributed to the respective respondents. Based on the feedback from questionnaires returned, only 143 were completed, or about an 83 percent return rate, to be analyzed to generate the study findings. It describes the demographic characteristics and background of the respondents and examines the variables used in the data collection. This chapter will provide the input to formulate chapter 5.

The findings are presented according to the objectives of the study beginning with the reliability test results, answering objectives, and hypothesis test. The analyzed data are presented in the form of tables and figures. *Statistical Package For Social Sciences* (SPPS) Version 19.0 for Windows was applied to conduct the entire analysis, such as descriptive analysis and inferential statistics. Based on the result of the reliability test, the methodology and variables applied in this study were found reliable with Cronbach's alpha value of 0.965, which is bigger than 0.6000. This means that the variables applied in this study can be accepted because of their internal consistency. The closer the alpha is to 1.0, the higher the internal reliability of the item. The alpha value that falls below 0.6 is considered questionable, while the Cronbach's alpha value that falls above 0.7 can be accepted. The alpha value that is higher than 0.8 is considered good (Hair et al. 2007). Therefore, the minimum alpha value that has been set for this study is 0.7.

4.2   Profile of the Respondent

The demographic backgrounds of the respondents were taken into much consideration in this study, as they are believed to influence their attitude toward the questions asked in the questionnaires, as stated in Sumbeh, 2010. Based on the findings, there were no biases or discrimination in distributing the questionnaires to the respondents. There were eight age groups among respondents who ranged from fewer than 25 to more than 56 years old. The distribution is widely equal across the group range. About 44.1 percent aged between 36 to 45 years old, followed by 17.5 percent for ages between 26 to 30 years old and 10 percent are aged fewer than 25 years old. The remaining were aged above 41 to more than 56 years old as shown in figure 4.1. The overall mean age group among the studied respondents is at 3.72, or at 36.71 years old, which are considered experienced enough in compliance to safety in a proper manner in their respective workplace.

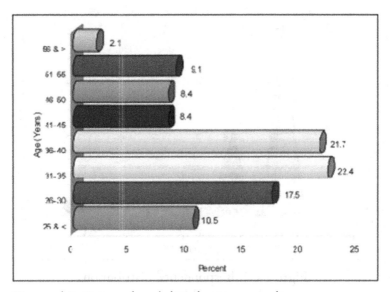

Figure 4.1: Respondents' distribution according to age group.

This finding was supported by statistics that revealed the total job experience in Brooke Dockyard recorded average at that six and a half years, with 59.47 percent of the respondents considered equipped with new experience at fewer than five years in delivering their respective task. Another 25.2 percent of the respondents have between six to ten years' experience, while the remaining 15.3 percent of them have experience for more than ten years as illustrated in figure 4. 2.

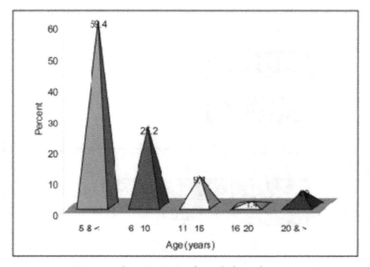

Figure 4.2: Respondents' distribution
according to working experiences.

In line with their hierarchy in job positions and working
experiences, there were slightly more than a quarter of respondents
having their undergraduate degree (28.7 percent). On the other
hand, the highest percentages at 53.8 percent were employees
with secondary schooling. Figure 4.3 shows the differences in
educational backgrounds.

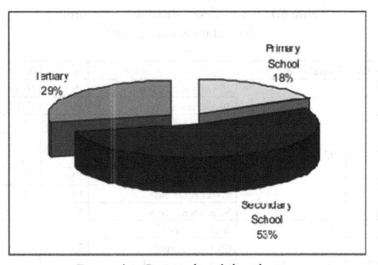

Figure 4.3: Respondents' distribution
according to educational level.

The entire respondents have attended OSH induction programs, which is contradictive with 9.3 percent never experiencing an accident at the workplace. The detail analysis on the demographic background is as shown in table 4.1.

Table 4.1: Respondents' distribution according to demographic background.

No	Variable		N	%
1	Age Group	25 years old & less	15	10.5
		26–30 years old	25	17.5
		31–35 years old	32	22.4
		36–40 years old	31	21.7
		41-45 years old	12	8.4
		46–50 years old	12	8.4
		51–55 years old	13	9.1
		56 years old & >	3	2.1
	Mean Age	36.71 years old		
2	Educational Level	Primary School	25	17.5
		Secondary School	77	53.8
		Tertiary	41	28.7
3	Ethnic Group	Malay	45	31.5
		Chinese	18	12.6
		Iban	44	30.8
		Bidayuh	20	14.0
		Others	15	15.05
		Foreign Worker	1	0.7
4	Working Experiences (years) in Brooke Dockyard	5 years & less	85	59.4
		6–10 years	36	25.2
		11–15 years old	13	9.1
		16–20 years	2	1.4
		More than 20 years	7	4.9
	Mean	6.5 years		
5	Attending Induction Course	Yes	143	100.0
		No	0	0
6	Experience of Accident at the Workplace	Yes	10	7.0
		No	133	93.0
7	Gender	Male	112	78.3
		Female	31	21.7
			143	**100**

4.3 Knowledge on OSH Induction Course

As the study focuses on safety and health compliance, it is necessary to identify the differences in the job groups. Almost a third, or 32.2 percent, of the respondents was from the Yard Fabrication Team, which was supported that Brooke Dockyard main activities and operations were dealing with fabrication works. Another job group revealed that almost a quarter, or 24.5 percent, was for Project Management Team (PMT) followed by HSE at 14.7 percent. The remaining were: Blasting/Painting Team (11.2 percent), Electrical and Instrument Team (7.0 percent), Yard Maintenance Team (7.0 percent), Scaffolding Team (2.1 percent), and Cranage Operation Team (1.4 percent). Running the organizational businesses at a large scale needs collaborations from various fields of expertise to ensure that the organizations' visions and missions are achieved.

Table 4.2: Respondents' distribution according to job group.

	Frequency	Percent
Project Management Team (PMT)	35	24.5
Blasting/Painting Team	16	11.2
Cranage Operation Team	2	1.4
Electrical & Instrument Team	10	7.0
Yard Fabrication Team	46	32.2
Scaffolding Team	3	2.1
Yard Maintenance Team	10	7.0
HSE	21	14.7
Total	143	100.0

For this section, the researcher seeks to evaluate respondents' knowledge on OSH Induction Course. There were twenty statements regarding the OSH Induction Course posed to them with multiple-choice answers. Each of the corrected answers was given five marks to accumulate 100 percent for the entire statements. Furthermore, the accumulated marks are to be divided into five groups as shown in table 4.3.

Table 4.3: Knowledge level.

Accumulated Marks	Knowledge Level
01 to 20	Poor
21 to 40	Little
41 to 60	Average
61 to 80	Good
81 to 100	Excellent

The descriptive statistics revealed that the mean scored for knowledge level on OSH among studied is at 77.34 with standard deviation of 10.9. Thus, the mean value is considered high, which is supported by mode (70.0) and median at (80.0). A comparison between the lowest mark and the highest mark found that the minimum scored is at 50.0 compared to the highest mark at 100.00. In line with the study objective, which was to determine the knowledge level on the OSH Induction Course, it is found that the entire respondents scored at least at the average level. Table 4.4 shows that about 68.5 percent of them scored Good followed by Excellent at 17.5 percent; the remaining at Average at 14.0 percent. This means that the entire respondents whom represented workers at Brooke Dockyard could be considered knowledgeable at various ranges as illustrated in figure 4.4. The detailed feedback for each statement is attached as appendix 3.

Table 4.4: Respondents' distribution according to knowledge level on OSH Induction Course.

	Frequency	Percent	Valid Percent	Cumulative Percent
Average	20	14.0	14.0	14.0
Good	98	68.5	68.5	82.5
Excellent	25	17.5	17.5	100.0
Total	143	100.0	100.0	

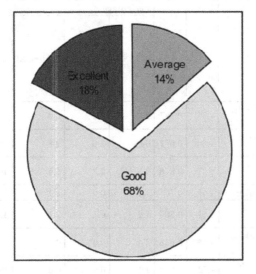

Figure 4.4: Respondents' distribution according to knowledge level on OHS Induction Course.

4.4 Organization Safety Management

The researcher seeks to determine the respondents' perception towards the organization safety management. There were ten statements in the organizational safety management section. Respondents' feedback shows that overall the mean value scored is ranging from 4.32 to 4.55 for the entire statements as shown in table 4.6 below. The highest mean scored were for the following two statements: "Provide safe working environments," and "Keeps workers informed of hazards," with the standard deviation of 0.767 respectively. A detailed analysis found that majority respondents at 97.2 percent gave positive feedback as shown in figure 4.5. Both statements indicated that the employees needed to be alerted, especially for changes or directives in the organization by the management team.

Table 4.5: Respondents' feedback for
organization safety management.

| Statement | Mean | SD | Percentage | | | | |
			Strongly Disagree	Disagree	Undecided	Agree	Strongly Agree
Provide enough safety programs	4.55	0.767	2.7	0.0	0.0	34.3	62.9
Conduct frequent safety inspection	4.34	0.672	0.0	2.8	2.8	51.7	42.7
Investigate safety problems quickly	4.37	0.878	2.8	2.8	1.4	40.6	52.4
Reward safe workers	4.46	0.767	1.4	0.0	1.4	42.7	54.5
Provide safe equipment	4.51	0.804	4.2	0.7	2.1	32.2	62.2
Provide safe working environments	4.46	0.648	2.4	0.0	0.0	45.5	51.7
Respond quickly to safety concerns	4.52	0.648	2.1	0.0	0.0	39.2	58.0
Help maintain clean work areas	4.32	0.765	2.8	0.0	9.8	39.9	47.6
Provide safety information	4.42	0.791	2.1	2.1	0.0	43.4	52.4
Keep workers informed of hazards	4.55	0.767	2.7	0.0	0.0	34.3	62.9

[N = 143, Mean = 4.56, and SD = 0.766.]

Based on the analysis, the lowest mean scored is for the following statement: "Help maintain clean work areas" at 4.32, with standard deviation of 0.765. About 43.4 percent agreed, and 47.6 percent strongly agreed with the statement, in contrast to 2.8 percent strongly disagreeing and 9.8 percent as undecided. This explained that the safest workers must be rewarded, and those committing OSH violations be penalized accordingly to prevent future violations.

In conclusion on the organizational safety management, the analysis revealed that the overall mean is at 4.56 and standard deviation at 0.766, which is high in the positive direction, and the total percentage scored for Agree and Strongly Agree for each statement is exceeding 80.0 percent, with 100 percent for five statements.

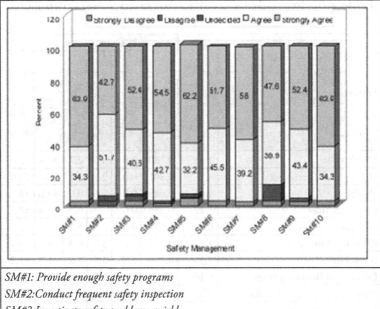

SM#1: Provide enough safety programs
SM#2:Conduct frequent safety inspection
SM#3:Investigate safety problems quickly
SM#4:Reward safe workers
SM#5:Provide safe equipment
SM#6:Provide safe working environments
SM#7:Respond quickly to safety concerns
SM#8:Help maintain clean work areas
SM#9:Provide safety information
SM#10:Keep workers informed of hazards

Figure 4.5: Respondents' feedback for organization safety management.

4.5   Safety Programs/Policies

The researcher seeks to determine the respondents' perception on safety programs or policies adopted by the organization. There were ten statements in this section. Respondents' feedback showed that overall the mean value scored ranged from 4.29 to 4.57 for the entire statements as shown in table 4.6 below. The highest mean scored is for the statement, "Help prevent accidents," with standard deviation of 0.801.

Table 4.6: Respondents' feedback for safety programs/policies.

| Statement | Mean | SD | Percentage | | | | |
			Strongly Disagree	Disagree	Undecided	Agree	Strongly Agree
Worthwhile	4.31	0.780	0.0	3.5	2.7	52.4	42.0
Helps prevent accidents	4.57	0.801	0.0	2.7	3.5	26.6	67.8
Useful	4.41	0.685	0.0	5.6	0.0	44.8	49.7
Good Practices	4.42	0.686	0.0	4.9	0.7	44.4	50.3
First-Rate	4.29	0.810	0.0	2.8	5.6	49.0	42.7
Clear & Visionary	4.42	0.834	0.0	3.5	6.3	35.7	55.9
Important	4.35	0.790	0.0	2.8	2.8	48.3	46.2
Effective in Reducing Injuries	4.40	0.832	0.0	2.7	7.0	37.8	53.8
Must Apply to My Workplace	4.51	0.730	0.0	0.7	9.3	29.4	62.2
Fully Functioning	4.40	0.725	0.0	6.2	3.5	39.2	52.4

[N = 105, Mean = 4.64, and SD = .791]

An in-depth analysis by the researcher found that the contributing factors to high positive feedback due to knowledge and understanding on safety programs/policies applied in the organization. The researcher thinks that it is important for each employee to know this aspect, as positive responses from the individual could be considered as a supporting factor contributed to high safety compliance. Also, this statement was to prove that short-term and long-term safety programs, or training for employees, was highly needed.

In conclusion on safety programs/policies, the analysis revealed that the overall mean is at 4.64 and standard deviation at 0.791, which is high in the positive direction. Figure 4.6 below shows the total percentage scored for Agree and Strongly Agree for each statement exceeding 85.0 percent.

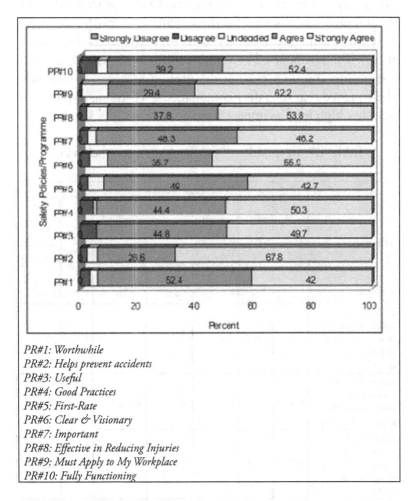

PR#1: *Worthwhile*
PR#2: *Helps prevent accidents*
PR#3: *Useful*
PR#4: *Good Practices*
PR#5: *First-Rate*
PR#6: *Clear & Visionary*
PR#7: *Important*
PR#8: *Effective in Reducing Injuries*
PR#9: *Must Apply to My Workplace*
PR#10: *Fully Functioning*

Figure 4.6: Respondents' feedback for safety programs/policies.

4.6   Perception on Safety Behavior

For this variable, the researcher seeks to find the safety behavior of the respondents on the degree of control over the behavior. Table 4.7 below shows that the mean scored for the entire statement ranged from 2.40 to 4.47, which means the majority of the respondents who gave positive feedback either agree or strongly agree with the statements given. On the other hand, a low mean scored was observed for the statement, "Only follow safety rules that I think are necessary" at 2.40, with standard deviation of 1.37. This is supported by almost a third, or 35 percent, strongly disagreeing and 24.5 percent disagreeing as negative feedback. These proved that the safety compliance level among respondents were at a high level as impact from attending OSH Courses.

Table 4.7: Respondents' feedback on safety behavior.

Statement	Mean	SD	Percentage				
			Strongly Disagree	Disagree	Undecided	Agree	Strongly Agree
Don't overlook safety procedures in order to get my job done more quickly.	4.46	0.870	2.8			67.1	30.1
Follow all safety procedures regardless of the situation I am in.	4.43	0.765	1.4	1.4	2.8	34.3	60.1
Handles all situations as if there is a possibility of having an accident.	4.30	0.741	2.1		0.7	45.5	51.7

	Mean	SD					
Wear my safety equipment required by practice.	4.42	0.800	3.5			58.0	38.5
Encourage my coworkers to be safe.	4.35	0.790	3.5	0.7	2.8	41.3	53.1
Keep my work equipment in a safe working environment.	4.45	0.76	2.8			44.1	53.1
Do not take shortcuts in order to get my job done faster.	4.47	0.767	1.4	1.4		42.0	55.5
Only follow safety rules that I think are necessary.	2.40	1.37	35.0	24.5	18.2	10.5	11.9
Report safety problems to my supervisor when I see safety problems.	4.30	0.814	2.1		6.3	47.6	44.1
Correct safety problems to ensure accidents will not occur.	4.46	0.766		3.5		32.2	64.3

[N = 143, Mean = 4.22, and SD = .713]

The highest mean scored is at 4.47 for the statement, "Do not take shortcuts in order to get my job done faster," which scored 42.0 percent for Agree and 55.5 percent for Strongly Agree. In contrast, about 1.4 percent of respondents claimed that "undecided". In this regard, an in-depth analysis was made, and the researcher identified that the worker's component as the main factor that influence the responds, where each employee tried to ensure that their colleague is conducting their task in safety environment. The remaining statements also indicated a high mean value, which skewed toward a positive direction. Hence, the researcher concludes that respondents show high levels of positive feedback with regards to their safety behaviors.

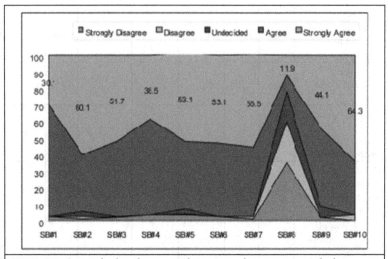

SB#1: *Don't overlook safety procedures in order to get my job done more quickly.*

SB#2: *Follow all safety procedures regardless of the situation I am in.*

SB#3: *Handles all situations as if there is a possibility of having an accident.*

SB#4: *Wear my safety equipment required by practice.*

SB#5: *Encourage my coworkers to be safe.*

SB#6: *Keep my work equipment in a safe working environment.*

SB#7: *Do not take shortcuts in order to get my job done faster.*

SB#8: *Only follow safety rules that I think are necessary.*

SB#9: *Report safety problems to my supervisor when I see safety problems.*

SB#10: *Correct safety problems to ensure accidents will not occur.*

Figure 4.7: Respondents' distribution according to feedback on safety behavior.

4.7   Pearson's Correlation Analysis

In line with the objectives of the study, the Pearson's Correlation analysis was conducted to investigate the relationship within the studied variables. First was between the demographic backgrounds with the independent variables, and second was within independent variables. At 95 percent, confident level was applied as a guideline to conduct the analysis.

The statistic shown in table 4.9 revealed that none of the demographic variables has significant relationship with the study's construct, which proved by the significance (*p* value) at 95 percent confident level is higher than 0.05. For example, an in-depth analysis found that the differences in age group among respondents *does not influence* their perception or feedback on perception on organization safety management (p = 0.888, r = 0.012) or safety programs/policies (p = 0.763, r = -0.025) in negative relationship and safety compliance (p = 0.167, r = 0.116). The negative direction explained that respondents within a younger age group were more compliant compared to the older age groups. This is supported by years of experience and the older age group tending to have a static mind-set and not willing to change—while the younger have the tendency to comply with the safety requirement.

The second demographic variable is the educational level among respondents. Overall, there are no significant relationships between educational levels with study constructs. This was proved that their perception on organization safety management (p = 0.632, r = -0.040), safety programs/policies (p = 0.405, r = -0.070) in negative relationships, and safety compliance (p = 0.667, r = -0.0366). These means the differences in educational background did *not* influenced their feedback on the study constructs. Working experiences in the fabrication industry recorded no significant relationship, as other demographic backgrounds which are no significant relationship existed between variables.

Table 4.8: Pearson's Correlations Analysis between demographic background and study construct.

		Knowledge Level on OSS	Organization Safety Management	Safety Programs or policies	Behavior at Workplace
Age Group	Pearson's Correlation	.010	.012	-.025	.116
	Sig. (2-tailed)	.910	.888	.763	.167
	N	143	143	143	143
Educational Level	Pearson's Correlation	.045	-.040	-.070	-.036
	Sig. (2-tailed)	.590	.632	.405	.667
	N	143	143	143	143
Working Experience	Pearson's Correlation	-.016	.082	.002	.106
	Sig. (2-tailed)	.846	.329	.981	.207
	N	143	143	143	143
Experience Accident at the workplace	Pearson's Correlation	-.032	-.122	.085	-.109
	Sig. (2-tailed)	.706	.145	.315	.194
	N	143	143	143	143
Gender	Pearson's Correlation	-.033	-.074	-.042	-.041
	Sig. (2-tailed)	.697	.377	.620	.626
	N	143	143	143	143

Table 4.9 shows the relationships within the study constructs component. The statistics revealed that respondents' perception for knowledge on an OSH Induction recorded no significant relationship with perception on organization safety management ($p = 0.003$, $r = 0.969$) and safety programs/policies ($p = 0.368$, $r = 0.076$) in positive direction, whereas safety behaviors at the workplace ($p = 0.057$, $r = -0.160$). This means their perception of safety management, safety programs/policies, and behaviors at the workplace were not influenced or determined by their knowledge level on OSH among the workers.

On the other hand, perception on safety management recorded a significant relationship with safety programs/policies (p = 0.623, r = 0.000) and safety behaviors at the workplace (p = 0.692, r = 0.00). The explanation showed that respondents with high knowledge on organization management influenced his/her behavior at the workplace. To support that relationship between policies/programs also recorded a significant relationship in positive direction with behaviors at the workplace. Hence, the researcher concludes that with high knowledge on organization safety management and policies adopted by the respective organization has a determinant factor for respondents to be compliant at the workplace.

Table 4.9: Pearson's Correlations Analysis
within main components.

		Knowledge Level on OSH	Organization Safety Management	Safety Programs/ Policies	Safety Behavior at Workplace
Knowledge Level on OSH	Pearson's Correlation	1			
	Sig. (2-tailed)				
	N	143			
Organization Safety Management	Pearson's Correlation	.003	1		
	Sig. (2-tailed)	.969			
	N	143	143		
Safety Programs/ Policies	Pearson's Correlation	.076	.623**	1	
	Sig. (2-tailed)	.368	.000		
	N	143	143	143	
Safety Behavior at Workplace	Pearson's Correlation	-.160	.692**	.600**	1
	Sig. (2-tailed)	.057	.000	.000	
	N	143	143	143	143

**. Correlation is significant at the 0.01 level (2-tailed).

4.8 Restatement of Research Hypotheses

The purpose of the restatement of research hypotheses is to prove the research framework. In this research, the one-way

ANOVA was applied to investigate the significant level (p) to determine the acceptance of the tested hypotheses. A significant p-value resulting from a one-way ANOVA test would indicate that a perception is differentially expressed in at least one of the groups analyzed. If there are more than two groups being analyzed, however, the one-way ANOVA does not specifically indicate which pair of groups exhibits statistical differences. Whereas, a t-test applied for the two variables for the study constructs. An in-depth analysis was conducted to investigate the respondents' perceptions based on their demographic backgrounds. There were seven variables in the demographic backgrounds that have been selected for the purposes of this study. Four of the variables in the demographic backgrounds have more than two variables; hence, one-way ANOVA was implemented, whereas the remaining variables adopted t-test analyses.

4.8.1 Significant differences for respondents' perception on safety compliance according to demographic background

First Hypothesis

H_{01a}:   *There is no significant difference in respondents' perception on safety compliance according to age group*

As shown in table 4.10a, the differences in the age group among respondents recorded no significant differences among respondents' perceptions on compliance of safety as impact on OSH Induction, which is proved by $p > 0.05$ at 95 percent confidence level for two-tailed analysis. Hence, this hypothesis should be accepted because the younger age groups have no differences in their perception about compliance of safety compared to the older groups among the studied respondents, or compliance of safety among respondents were not determine by their age group.

Table 4.10a: ANOVA for respondents' perception
on safety compliance according to age group.

	Sum of Squares	Df	Mean Square	F	Sig.
Between Groups	7.095	2	3.547	1.048	.353
Within Groups	473.716	140	3.384		
Total	480.811	142			

Second Hypothesis

H_{01b}: *There is no significant difference in respondents' perception on safety compliance according to educational level*

Similar patterns for academic backgrounds or educational levels among respondents recorded there was no significant between studied variables. Table 4.10b shows the significant level at 0.904 proves that the differences in respondents' academic qualifications were not the dominant factor that determined their perception on compliance of safety. This explained that respondents with lower educational levels also indicated high compliance of safety. A low academic educational level was not a factor to ignore safety requirement at the workplace. For example, for those who have difficulties reading and understanding the written rules and regulations, their team leader or supervisor are there to be their reference.

Table 4.10b ANOVA for respondents' perception on
safety compliance according to educational level.

	Sum of Squares	Df	Mean Square	F	Sig.
Between Groups	.092	2	.046	.101	.904
Within Groups	64.117	140	.458		
Total	64.210	142			

Third Hypothesis

H_{01c}: *There is no significant difference in respondents' perception on safety compliance according to number of years' experience working in oil at Brooke Dockyard*

A third hypothesis is experience working in the oil and gas industry. The statistic as per table 4.10c shows that their compliance of safety recorded no significant difference with significant value at 0.493, which explained the number of years' experience working in fabrication industry does not influence their perception on compliance of safety. This revealed that respondents with greater number of years' experience in the oil and gas industry gave almost similar feedback to the lesser experience. This is due to the orientation imposed by the organization, which ensures that each employee must follow the policies adopted by the organization.

Table 4.10c: ANOVA for respondents' perception on safety compliance according to number of years' working experience.

	Sum of Squares	Df	Mean Square	F	Sig.
Between Groups	54.429	2	27.215	.711	.493
Within Groups	5355.603	140	38.254		
Total	5410.032	142			

Fourth Hypothesis

H_{01d}: *There is no significant difference in the respondents' perception on safety compliance according to their gender group.*

For this hypothesis, a t-test analysis was conducted with the results shown in table 4.10d. The results show that p < 0.05, meaning there is significant difference existing between perception on compliance of safety and their gender group. The H_{01e} have to be rejected due to the significant level at p = 0.00 at 95 percent confidence level for two-tailed analysis. This indicates that the respondents' perception on compliance of safety was determined by their gender in the study organization. This explained that females have less compliance of safety level compared to male workers due to their differences in nature of work when exposed to hazards.

Table 4.11d: T-test for respondents' perception on safety compliance according to their gender group.

	t	df	Sig. (2-tailed)	Mean Difference	Lower	Upper
Safety	35.189	142	.000	1.217	1.15	1.29
Behavior	70.678	142	.000	4.217	4.10	4.33

Sixth Hypothesis

H_{02}: *There is no significant difference between knowledge on organization safety management with safety compliance among respondents*

The results show that $p < 0.05$, meaning there is a significant difference existing between perception on compliance of safety and their perception on organization safety management. The H_{02} have to be rejected because of the significant level at $p < 0.05$ at 95 percent confidence level for two-tailed analysis. This indicates that the respondents' perception on compliance of safety was determined by their perception level on organization safety management. This explains that respondents with high knowledge on safety management were highly compliant. This is supported by the argument that they know the dos and don'ts in their respective organizations.

Table 4.10e: ANOVA test for organization safety
management and safety compliance.

	Sum of Squares	Df	Mean Square	F	Sig.
Between Groups	53.577	2	26.788	126.412	.000
Within Groups	29.668	140	.212		
Total	83.245	142			

Seventh Hypothesis

H_{03}: *There is no significant difference between safety programs/
policies with safety compliance among respondents*

Table 4.10f shows the significant difference/level recorded
at 0.000 for the 95 percent confident level reveal that awareness
policies have influenced their perception on compliance of safety.
The result, $p < 0.05$, is enough to support the hypotheses to be
rejected. Respondents with greater awareness on safety compliance
gave feedback skewed to positive direction, which means high
awareness mean better performance of safety at worksite.

Table 4.11f: ANOVA test for safety policies/
programs and safety compliance.

	Sum of Squares	df	Mean Square	F	Sig.
Between Groups	54.625	2	27.313	111.851	.000
Within Groups	34.186	140	.244		
Total	88.811	142			

Eighth Hypothesis

H_{04}: *There is no significant difference between organization safety
management with policies/programs among respondents*

As observed for one-way ANOVA results between respondents'
perception on organization safety and safety/program level, there
is a significant difference between studied variables. Table 4.10g

shows that p < 0.05 suggested that this hypothesis to be rejected because of significant differences between studied respondents. High commitment is one driving factor to ensure comprehensive implementation of safety at the workplace.

Table 4.10g: ANOVA test for organization safety management and policies/programs.

	Sum of Squares	Df	Mean Square	F	Sig.
Between Groups	54.625	2	27.313	111.851	.000
Within Groups	34.186	140	.244		
Total	88.811	142			

Ninth Hypothesis

H_{05}: *There is no significant difference between knowledge on OSH Induction Course with safety compliance among respondents*

Finally, the one-way ANOVA analysis between respondents' knowledge on OSH Induction Course with safety compliance recorded there is significant difference between studied variables. Table 4.10h shows that p < 0.05 suggests that this hypothesis to be rejected because of significant differences between studied respondents. High knowledge on OSH Induction Course motivates respondents to act as compliant to safety at workplace.

Table 4.10h: ANOVA test for knowledge on OSH Induction Course with safety compliance.

	Sum of Squares	df	Mean Square	F	Sig.
Between Groups	5.900	2	2.950	10.609	.000
Within Groups	38.926	140	.278		
Total	44.825	142			

4.9.1   Chapter Summary

This chapter has reported the findings of the study of the perception on OSH Induction Program in line to improve safety awareness. Overall findings showed that the majority of respondents indicated high level of knowledge on OSH Induction and similar pattern for the other study constructs. This was proven by high safety compliance among them.

Chapter 5

DISCUSSION

5.1 Introduction

This chapter will discuss the findings of the OSH Induction program, the implications, and the conclusion. The discussion will be based on the variables examined in the previous chapters.

5.2 Discussion

5.2.1 Demographic Characteristic

In line with their hierarchy in job position and working experiences, there were slightly more than a quarter of respondents having their undergraduate degree, whereas the remaining were primary and secondary school level. The entire respondents have attended an OSH Induction Program, which is in line to promote safety culture in the organization.

Relationships between demographic backgrounds with the study constructs found that the differences in demographic background among respondents does not influence their perception or feedback for knowledge level on OSH, organization safety management, safety programs/policies, and safety behavior toward safety at the workplace. For example, respondents from an older age group recorded that their knowledge level on OSH were almost similar to the younger age group's. This is supported by years of experience engaged by the studied organization, which indicates almost similar findings.

5.2.2 Knowledge on OSH Induction Program

Almost a third, or 32.2 percent, of the respondents were from the Yard Fabrication Team, supported by Brooke Dockyard main activities and operations were dealing with fabrication works. The descriptive statistic revealed that the mean scored for knowledge level on OSH amongst respondents is at 77.34, with standard deviation of 10.9. This means there was a high knowledge level, which is supported by mode (70.0) and median at (80.0). These means that the entire respondents whom represented workers at Brooke Dockyard could be considered knowledgeable at various ranges. This finding is in line with a study conducted by Giustina and Giustina (1989), illustrating three important contributions management can offer employees to improve safety in the workplace, such as knowledge and understanding of safe and healthy work practices: employees must be trained to identify present and potential hazards not only in the jobs they are performing but in jobs being performed nearby.

5.2.3 Organization Safety Management

The researcher found that the respondents' perception of the organization safety management that overall the mean value scored is ranging from 4.32 to 4.55 for the entire statements. The analysis revealed that the overall mean is at 4.56 and standard deviation at 0.766, which is high in the positive directions and the total percentage scored for Agree" and Strongly Agree for each statement exceeding 80.0 percent, with 100 percent for five statements. Flin (et al. 2002) stated that safety management, or practices by the organization, had been proven to validate whether the management safety commitment is being transmitted to others in the same organization. An excellent safety management does not work from just simply knowing the written statement of safety procedures and regulations, but it requires extra efforts on demonstrating the safety commitment. Gadd and Collins (2002) agreed that management was a key influence toward safety illustrated from their well-planned control of discipline, attitude, and behavior toward safety.

Mitchison and Papadakis (1999) have demonstrated that effective safety management improves the level of safety in an organization and thus can be seen to decrease damages and harm from incidents. These were supported by Mearns et al. (2003), who noted that safety climate is considered to be the precise indicator of overall safety culture, while safety management practices display the safety culture of top management; as a result, good safety management practices are reflected in enhanced safety climate of all employees. Yule (et al. 2007) concludes that employees' perception of dedicated management's commitment resulted in prevention of incident in workplace.

5.2.4 Safety Programs/Policies

The researcher seeks to determine the respondents' perception on safety programs or policies adopted by the organization. There were ten statements in this section. Respondents' feedback shows that overall the mean value scored ranges from 4.29 to 4.57 for the entire statements. To conclude on safety programs/policies, the analysis revealed that the overall mean is at 4.64 and standard deviation at 0.791, which is high in the positive direction. The total percentage scored for Agree and Strongly Agree for each statement exceeding 85.0 percent.

This finding is in line with Law (et al. 2006) who stated that safety training and safety policy were also essential determinants to enhance safety performance. *Safety training* is defined as, "knowledge of safety given to employees in order for them to work safely and with no danger to their well being." It is supported by Lin and Mills (2001) that clear policy statements and safety training play an important role in reducing accident rates. Huang (et al. 2006) summarized that the link between safety training and increased safety performance.

To enhance good safety environments, management should develop safety programs, such as safety training and precaution. This recommendation supports the study by Zohar (1980) where safety program effectiveness scored the highest safety climate measure. Hayes (et al. 1998) confirmed that there was significant relationship between safety compliance with safety awareness. Other studies by Gykye (2005) and Gykye and Salminen (2007) proved that employees who were satisfied with safety programs provided by the organization were more compliant with safety regulations. Safety training consists of job enrichment programs and skill training where employees are more concerned on promising career path. Furthermore, from job enrichment programs, employees will become multitasking workers and thus motivate and benefit employees and organization.

5.2.5   Perception on Safety Behavior

For this variable, the researcher seeks to find out the safety behavior of the respondents on the degree of control over the behavior. The mean scored for the entire statement ranged from 2.40 to 4.47, which means the majority of the respondents who gave positive feedback either agree or strongly agree with the statements given. As observed, a single statement with a low mean level (at which is supported by more than half) gave negative feedback. The researcher concludes that respondents show high levels of positive feedback with regards to their safety behavior.

Ambia (2010) highlighted in her study findings that when the management safety puts high commitment toward safety concerns, promotes safety, investigates safety problems promptly, and puts more effort on safety, the employees' safety behaviors will also increase; hence, their level of compliance with safety rules and regulations will also increase. According to Gyekye (2009), stated that well-trained employees were more satisfied and committed with their jobs.

Chapter 6
CONCLUSION AND RECOMMENDATION

6.1 Conclusion

The major purpose of this study is to determine the level of OSH awareness, which influences safety performance specifically on safety compliance at Brooke Dockyard, Kuching. Reliability coefficients of Cronbach's alpha appeared to be obtained higher than 0.7 for each study construct, suggesting that the research instruments were appropriate indicators of their respective construct. Correlation analysis was done to examine the relationship between study constructs. There were no significant relationships between study constructs with demographic backgrounds. While the remaining constructs, such as knowledge on OSH, safety management, and safety programs or policies, recorded significant relationship with safety behavior.

However, the strength of relationship varied, which was proved by the Pearson's coefficient, or (r) value. During the study period, the researcher found that the limitations of the study could probably be due to the very limited timeframe to implement and explore other factors, especially external ones contributed to the safety compliance. This study could be more efficient if the timeframe were allocated longer with wider factors put into the consideration.

The first objective had been achieved by identified knowledge levels as discussed in chapter 4.3. The result of a mandatory OSH Induction Program enhanced employees' OSH awareness, knowledge, skills, and competency. Briefly, the study finding shows that about 68.5 percent of them scored Good, followed by Excellent at 17.5 percent, and the remaining at Average at 14.0 percent. This means that the entire respondents whom represented workers at Brooke Dockyard could be considered knowledgeable at various ranges in delivering their respective tasks. The 14.0 percent of workers had indicated that they had average OSH knowledge; this group is the focus area for improvement in the near future.

The second objective was achieved through Pearson's correlation analysis and restatement hypotheses of the study. The impact of training programs contributed to high compliance in OSH rules and regulations at the place of work. With the high OSH knowledge and skills, employees can mitigate OSH risks and high potential hazards proactively, thus preventing and minimizing injuries and occupational illnesses and serious incidences, which, in turn, creates conducive working environments for the fabrication activities. It is the organization's vision that one day OSH knowledge and skills will develop into a decent OSH culture within the organization.

6.2   Recommendations to Brooke Dockyard

Brooke Dockyard has established a set of rules and regulations at the place of work to comply with the legislation requirements, and there are still violations once in a while when supervision enforcement are lacking. OSH Induction Program is an excellent venue to create awareness and start compliance, but visible supervision, monitoring, intervention, and enforcement must be carried continuously to ensure maximum compliance and ensure decent and positive OSH culture is practiced consciously. Culture change takes time.

The practicing of cooperation, participation, and consultation by management and workers' representatives as outlined in the regulation while engaging in OSH Induction Program in the workplace is one way of achieving collaborating roles. OSH Induction Program is a mandatory for each employee, and management commitment is essential with the element of OSH management. This approach must be adopted when dealing with external parties as well. Effective coaching, guiding, and monitoring of OSH activities in the workplace were practiced during this study as well as focusing on the high-potential incidents. This approach shall be continued, improved, and changed if necessary.

Communication is one of the elements in an OSH management system. Effective communication and deliberation must be regularly adopted and practiced to ensure OSH knowledge and skills cascade and reach the employees. Any employee buy-in is a good win-win situation and should be optimized and maximized to achieve OSH objectives, targets, and continual improvement.

It has been said and publicized that OSH is good for business. Organizations that have good OSH practices and/or culture tend to have good businesses. It is suggested that the study could be carried out amongst the organizations that practice good OSH culture to determine and validate whether good OSH is good for business.

6.3   Recommendation for Future Study

Andrew Ronggie (2012) would like to recommend the following for future research:

1. Proposed to broaden the scope of study to include other fabrication industries.
2. Conduct the survey for a longer duration to get a better and more accurate response from the survey population.
3. Conduct study to cover both corporate employee and contractor community.

References

Alliger, M. G., and A. E. Janak. "Kirkpatrick's Levels of Training Criteria: Thirty Years Later." *Personnel Psychology* 42, no. 2 (1989): 331–342.

Alliger, M. G., I. S. Tannenbaum, W. Bennett, H. Traver, and A. Shotland. "A Meta-Analysis of the Relations among Training Criteria." *Personnel Psychology* 50, no. 2 (1997): 341–358.

Anderson, J. C., M. Rungtusanatham, and R. G. Schroeder. "A Theory of Quality Management Underlying the Deming Management Method." *Academy of Management Review* 19, no. 3 (1994): 472–509.

Barrow, C. J. *Social Impact Assessment: An Introduction*. New York: Oxford University Press, 2000.

Brauer, R. L. *Safety and Health for Engineers*. New York: Van Nostrand Reinhold, 1990.

Bloom, B. *Taxonomy of Educational Objectives: The Cognitive Domain*. Donald Mckay: New York, 1956.

Bottani, E., L. Monica, and G. Vignali. "Safety Management Systems: Performance Differences between Adopters and Non-Adopters." *Safety Science* 47 (2009): 155–162.

Cheyne, A., A. Oliver, J. M. Tomas, and S. Cox. "The Architecture of Employee Attitudes to Safety in the Manufacturing Sector. *Personnel Review* 31 (2002): 649–670.

Chua, Y. P. *Kaedah Penyelidikan - Kaedah dan Statistik Penyelidikan - Buku 1*, McGraw Hill Education, Kuala Lumpur, 2006.

Cooper, R. D., and S. P. Schindler. *Business Research Methods* (10th Edition). McGray-Hill/Irwin: New York, 2008.

Cronbach, L. J. "Coefficient Alpha and the Internal Structure of Tests." *Psychometrika* 16 (1951): 297–334.

Doll, R., and R. Peto. "The Causes of Cancer: Quantifiable Estimates of Avoidable Risks of Cancer in the United States Today." *Journal of the National Cancer Institute* 66, no. 6 (1981): 1191–308.

Duff, A. R., and others. "Improving Safety by the Modification Behavior." *Construction Management and Economics* 12 (1981): 67–78.

Fitts, P. M. *Perceptual-motor Skills Learning*. New York: Academic Press, 1964.

Gadd S., and A.M. Collins. "Safety Culture: A Review of the Literature Health and Safety Laboratory." *Health and Safety Laboratory*, 2002.

Gagne, M. R. "Learning Outcomes and Their Effects: Useful Categories of Human Performance." *American Psychologist* 39, no. 4 (1984): 377–385.

Giustina, J. L.d., and Giustina, D.E. "Quality of Work Life Program Through Employee Motivation." *Professional Safety* 34, no. 5 (1989): 24–28.

Glendon, A, I., and N. A. Stanton. "Perspectives on Safety Culture." *Safety Science* 34 (2000):193–214.

Goldstein, I. L. *Training in Organizations: Needs Assessment, Development, and Evaluation* (3rd ed.). Pacific Grove, CA: Brooks/Cole Publishing Company, 1983.

Goldstein, L. I., and J. K. Ford. "Training in Organizations: Needs Assessment, Development, and Evaluation (4th ed.). Belmont, CA.: Wadsworth Publishing, 2002.

Griffin, M., and A. Neal. "Perceptions Safety at Work: A Framework for Linking Safety Climate to Safety Performance, Knowledge, and Motivation." *Journal of Occupational Health Psychology* 5 (2002): 347–358.

Grimaldi, J. V., and R. H. Simonds. *Safety Management* (5th ed.). Boston: Homewood, 1989.

Giustina, J. L.d., and Danier E.D. Giustina. "Quality of Work Life Program Through Employee Motivation." *Professional Safety* 34, no. 5 (1989): 24–28.

Gyekye, A. S. "Perceptions of Workplace Safety: Perception from Miners and Nonminers." *Professional Safety* (2006): 34–40.

Gyekye, A. S., and S. Salminen. "Making Sense of Industrial Accidents: The Role of Job Satisfaction." *Journal of Social Sciences* 2, no. 4 (2006): 127–134.

Hair, J. F. Jr., A. H. Money, P. Samouel, and M. Page. *Research Methods for Business*. United Kingdom: John Wiley and Son Ltd., 2007..

Ibid.

Hale, A. R. "Culture Confusions." *Safety Science* 34, nos. 1–3 (2007): 1–14.

Hayes, B., J. Perander, T. Smecko, J. Trask. "Measuring Perceptions of Workplace Safety: Development and Validation of the Work Safety Scale." *Journal of Society Research* 29 (1998): 145–161.

Hahn, S. E., and L. R. Murphy. "A Short Scale for Measuring Safety Climate." *Safety Science* 46 (2008): 1,047–1,066

Health and Safety Executive (HSE). "Safety Culture: A Review of the Literature." Retrieved on 7 June 2012: http://www.hse.gov.uk/research/hsl_pdf/2002/hsl02-25.pdf. (2007).

Heinrich, H.W., D. Peterson, and N. Roos. *Industrial Accident Prevention.* New York: McGraw-Hill, 1980.

Hinze, J., D. Bren, and N. Piepho. "Experience Modification Rating as Measure of Safety Performance." *Journal of Construction Engineering and Management* 121, no. 4 (1995): 455–458.

Hofmann, D. A., and F. P. Morgeson. "Safety-Related Behaviour as a Social Exchange: The Role of Perceived Organizational Support and Leader-Member Exchange." *Journal of Applied Psychological* 84, no. 2 (1999): 286–296.

Hsu, S. L., C. M. Wu, and K. Takano. "A Cross-Cultural Study of Organizational Factors on Safety: Japanese vs. Taiwanese Oil Refinery Plants." *Accident Analysis and Prevention* 40 (2008): 24–34.

Huang, Y, H., M. Ho, G. S. Smith, and P. Y. Chen. "Safety Climate and Self-Reported Injury: Assessing the Mediating Role of Employee Safety Control." *Accident Analysis and Prevention* 38 (2006): 425–433.

Health and Safety Executive. *Review of the Occupational Health and Safety of Britain's Ethnic Minorities*. Research Report 221, Suffolk: HSE Books, 2004.

Ibid, Research Report 510.

Health and Safety Executive. *An Empirical Analysis of the Effect of Health on Aggregate Income and Individual Labour Market Outcomes in the UK*. Research Report 639, Suffolk: HSE Books, 2008.

Ilmarinen, J., J. Rutenfranz, P. Knauth, M. Ahrens, H. Kylian, and U. Korallus. "The Effect of an On the Job Training Program—Stairclimbing—on the Physical Working Capacity of Employees." *European Journal of Applied Physiology and Occupational Physiology* 38 (1978): 25–40.

International Labour Office. *Safety Culture at Work. Safety in Numbers: Pointers for a Global Safety Culture at Work*. Geneva: International Labour Office, 2003.

International Labour Office. *Introductory Report: Decent Work—Safe Work*. Geneva: International Labour Office, 2005.

International Labour Office. *Occupation Safety and Health Country Profiles*. Geneva: International Labour Office, 2006.

International Labour Office. *Beyond Death and Injuries: The ILO's Role in Promoting Safe and Healthy Jobs*. Geneva: International Labour Organization, 2008.

International Labour Office. *Occupational Safety and Health: Guideline on Occupational Safety and Health Management Systems*. Geneva, Switzerland: 2001.

Johnson, S. "Management Accountability for Safety Performance." *Professional Safety* 33, no. 6 (1988): 23–26.

Kelloway, E. K., and L. Francis. *Management of Occupational Health & Safety* (4th ed.). Ontario: Nelson Education Ltd., 2008.

Kraiger, K., J. K. Ford, and E. Salas. "Application of Cognitive, Skill-Based, and Affective Theories of Learning Outcomes to New Methods of Training Evaluation." *Journal of Applied Psychology* 78 (1993): 311–328.

Krathwohl, D. R., B. S. Bloom, and B. B. Masia. *Taxonomy of Educational Objectives: The Classification of Educational Goals.* White Plains, NY: Longman, 1964.

Law, W. K., A. H. S. Chan, and K. F. Pun. "Prioritising the Safety Management Elements: a Hierarchical Analysis for Manufacturing Enterprises," *Industrial Management & Data Systems* 106. no. 6 (2006): 778–792.

Law of Malaysia. *Occupational Safety and Health, Act 1994 (Act 514) and Regulations and Order.* Kuala Lumpur: International Law Book Services, 2000.

Law of Malaysia. *Factory and Machinery Act 1967 (Act 139) and Regulations and Orders.* Kuala Lumpur: International Law Book Services, 2000.

Lin, J., and A. Mills. "Measuring the Occupational Health and Safety Performance of Construction Companies in Australia. *Facilities* 19, nos. 3–4 (2001): 131–138.

Marsh, T. W., I. T. Robertson, A. R. Duff, R. A. Phillips, M. D. Cooper, and A. Weyman. "Improving Safety Behavior

Using Goal Setting and Feedback. *Leadership & Organization Development Journal* 16, no. 1 (1995): 5–12.

Mearns, K., R. Flin, M. Fleming, R. Gordon. *Human and Organisational Factors in Offshore Safety*. Sudbury: HSE Books, 1997.

Mearns, K., R. Flin, R. Gordon, M. Fleming. *Measuring Safety Climate on Offshore Platforms*, 1998.

Meams, K., S. M. Whitaker, and R. Flin. "Safety Climate, Safety Management Practice and Safety Performance in Offshore Environments." *Safety Science* 41, no. 8 (2003): 641–680.

Miller, D. C. *Handbook of Research Design and Social Measurement* (5ᵗʰ ed.). Sage, California: Newbury Park, 1991.

Mohd Majid Konting. *Kaedah Penyelidikan Pendidikan*. Dewan Bahasa dan Pustaka, Kuala Lumpur, 2005.

Morgan, B. R., and J. W. Casper. "Examining the Factor Structure of Participant Reactions to Training: A Multidimensional Approach." *Human Resource Development Querterly* 11, no. 3 (2000): 301–317.

Ng. S.T. et. al. *A Framework for Evaluating the Safety Performance of Construction Contractors*. Building and Environmental Article in Press, 2002: 1–9.

Nicole, D., and Pearl German. "Safety Practices in Construction Industry." *Professional Safety* 34, no. 1 (1988): 33–38.

Noe, A. R., and N. Schmitt. "The Influence of Trainee Attitudes on Training Effectiveness: Test of a Model." *Personnel Psychology* 39, no. 3 (1986): 497–523.

Occupational Safety and Health Act (OSHA). (Act 514) *and Regulations and Orders.* Kuala Lumpur: MCD Publishers Sdn. Bhd, 1994.

O'Toole, M. "The Relationship Between Employees' Perceptions of Safety and Organizational and Culture." *Journal of Safety Research* 33 (2002): 231–243.

Pallant, J. *SPSS Survival Manual. A Step-by-Step Guide to Data Analysis Using SPSS for Windows* (Version 15, 3rd ed.). NSW, Australia: Allen & Unwin, 2002.

Petersen, D. *Techniques of Safety Management.* New York: McGraw Hill Co., 1984.

Petersen, D. "Leadership and Safety Excellence: A Positive Culture Drives Performance." *Professional Safety Oct.* Edition, 2004: 28–32.

Ratnawills Md. Ambia. "Understanding Employees Compliance with Safety Behaviour in a telecommunication Industry." Masters' Thesis. Sintok: University Utara Malaysia, 2010.

Rekus, J. F. "Is Your Safety Training Program Effective?" *Occupational Hazards* 8 (1999): 38–40.

Rosenbaum, A. D., and A. R. Carlson. "Acquisition of Intellectual and Perceptual-Motor Skill." *Annual Review of Psychology* 52 (2001): 453–470.

Ruona, E. A. W., M. Leimbach, F. E. Holton III, and R. Bate., "The Relationship Between Learner Utility Reactions and Predicted Learning Transfer Amongst Trainees." *International Journal of Training and Development* 6, no. 4 (2002): 218–228.

Saari, M. L., R. T. Johnson, D. S. Mclaughlin, and M. D. Zimmerle. "A Survey of Management Training and Education Practice in U.S. Companies." *Personnel Psychology* 41, no. 4 (1988): 731–743.

Sekaran, U. *Research Methods for Business: A Skill-Building Approach* (4ᵗʰ ed.). New York: John Wiley & Sons, 2005.

Singleton, R., and Straits, B.C., *Approaches to Social Research* (4ᵗʰ ed). New York: Oxford University Press, 2005.

Snoddy, S. G. "Learning and Stability: A Psychophysiological Analysis of a Case of Motor Learning with Clinical Applications." *Journal of Applied Psychology* 10, no. 1 (1926): 136–145.

Sumbeh, K. "Perception on Long Learning Programme in Secondary School." Debak District in Sarawak. Master Thesis Unpublished. University Technology Malaysia (2010).

Tan, A. J., J. R. Hall, and C. Boyce. "The Role of Employee Reactions in Predicting Training Effectiveness." *Human Resource Development Quarterly* 14, no. 4 (2003): 397–411.

Warr, P., and D. Bunce. "Trainee Characteristics and Outcomes of Open Learning." *Personnel Psychology* 48 (1995): 347–375.

Ibid,, 48, no. 2: 347–375.

Vassie, L. H., and W. R. Lucas. "An Assessment of Health and Safety Management within Working Groups in the UK Manufacturing Sector." *Journal of Safety Research* 32, no. 4 (2001): 479–490.

Yule, S., R. Flin, and A. Murdy. "The Role of Management and Safety Climate in Preventing Risk-Taking at Work."

International Journal of Risk Assessment and Management 7, no. 2 (2007): 137–151.

Zikmund, WG. *Business Research Methods* (7ᵗʰ ed.). South-Western, Ohio, 2003.

Zohar, D. "Safety Climate in Industrial Organizations: Theoretical and Applied Implications." *Journal of Applied Psychology.* 65 (1980): 96–102.

Appendix 1

Permit to Work (PTW)

<table>
<tr><td colspan="3"></td><td>BDE-HSE-WI-014
Attachment 2
Revision No.: 2
Page 1 of 2</td></tr>
<tr><td colspan="4" align="center">BROOKE DOCKYARD AND ENGINEERING WORKS CORPORATION
PERMIT TO WORK FORM

Serial No.: ....</td></tr>
</table>

ACTIVITY AND WORK DESCRIPTION

☐ CONFINED SPACE ENTRY/ WORK	☐ HYDROTESTING / RE-INSTATEMENT WORK	☐ COMMISSIONING
☐ BLASTING/ PAINTING	☐ EXCAVATION	☐ SYSTEM NO.
☐ HEAVY/ SPECIAL LIFTING	☐ ELECTRICAL / INSTRUMENTATION	☐ SUB SYSTEM NO.
☐ RADIOGRAPHY (Attach RPO Checklist)	☐ SKIDDING/ WEIGHING	☐ TAG
☐ SCAFFOLDING ERECTION/DISMANTLING	☐ WORK OVER WATER	☐ OTHERS (Please specify)
☐ CHEMICAL CLEANING	☐ WELDING / GOUGING	....
☐ CUTTING / GRINDING	☐ PWHT	....

BRIEF DESCRIPTION OF WORK

AREA :	TIME START :	VALIDITY :
DATE :	COMPLETION TIME :	

PERSONAL PROTECTIVE EQUIPMENT (PPE) & SAFETY REQUIREMENT

☐ HELMETS/BOOTS	☐ BREATHING PROTECTION	☐ VENTILATION
☐ EYE/FACE PROTECTION	☐ COVERALLS	☐ BARRICADE / SAFETY SIGNBOARDS
☐ GLOVES	☐ SAFETY HARNESS	☐ CONFINE SPACE ENTRY CERTIFICATE NO.
☐ RADIOGRAPH PROTECTION	☐ GAS TEST	☐ ELECTRICAL ISOLATION CERT. NO.
☐ HEARING PROTECTION	☐ FIRE EXTINGUISHER	☐ MECHANICAL ISOLATION CERT. NO.

HAZARD IDENTIFICATION AND CONTROLS

HAZARDS	CONTROL (S)

SUPPORTING DOCUMENT (S) (please tick appropriately or add in as required)

1.	Procedure c/w Drawing		6	List of personnel involved	
2.	NDT Report		7	Heavy Lifting Releease Note	
3.	Works Instruction		8	Heavy Safety Check List	
4.	Equipment Register		9		
5.	JHA/JSA		10		

1. APPLICATION by Foreman /Supervisor	2. AUTHORISATION by Project Manager
I hereby agreed to carry out the abovesaid work and comply with all PPE, safety equipments and hazards controls listed above.	I hereby authorise the work to be carried out as per requirement.
Signature	Signature
Name	Name
Position	Position
Date/Time:	Date/Time:

3. ENDORSEMENT by HSE/Safety Person	4. APPROVAL by Construction Supt.
I hereby confirmed that I had visited & inspected the worksite and work can proceed as per requirements.	I visited the worksite, certified that the area is safe and approved the said work to be carried out.
Signature :	Signature :
Name :	Name :
Position :	Position :
Date/Time :	Date/Time:

4. COMPLETION DECLARATION BY Applicant & Constrcution Supt.	
I declare that the work had been completed and all housekeeping had been completed.	I had visited the work area and declared that housekeeping is satisfactory.
Applicant Signature :	Construction Supt. Signature :
Completion Date :	Completion Date :
Completion Time :	Completion Time :

NOTE :
1. All PTW to be submitted by cut-off time 7:00 p.m.
2. New PTW shall be re-applied for work beyond cut-off time.
3. Applicant must display signed PTW at Worksite for verification.

Appendix 2

Letter of Appointment

ANDREW ANAK RONGGIE (*Matrix No.: MD 091011*)
Executive Master in OSH Management (EMOSH), UTM.
c/o: Brooke Dockyard and Engineering Works Corporation
Lot 343, Block 8, MTLD Sejingkat, Jln. Bako, 93050 Kuching, Sarawak
Tel: 082-432817 HP: 012-8085709   07-April -2012

Acting General Manager
Brooke Dockyard and Engineering Works Corporation
Sublot 47-49, 1st to 3rd Flr, Blk A, Demak Laut Commercial Centre
Jalan Bako, 93050 Kuching, Sarawak

For kind attention of **Puan Norhizan Sazali** ,

Request for permission to carry out a study on OSH Induction Programme in Enhancing Safety Awareness Amongst Fabrication Workers/Personnel in Brooke Dockyard and Engineering Works Corporation, Kuching, Sarawak .

With reference to the subject above.

Study had shown that OSH Induction had shown positive factor in creating OSH awareness amongst the work force at the fabrication worksites in the country. However, this interaction had not been fully studied and reported. As one of the OSH student, I would like to carry out a study on OSH Induction Programme in enhancing safety awareness amongst fabrication workers in the Corporation's Yard.

The questionnaire attached herein required the fabrication workers/personnel to be respondent. The respondent is required to answer the Questionnaire attached. This questionnaire has no risk. Brief information pertaining to the questionnaire is included in the attachment.

I would appreciate very much if your goodself on behalf of the Corporation would grant permission to the fabrication workers/personnel to participate in answering the questionnaires to share their level of OSH awareness and knowledge so that induction programme could be assessed and designed to enhance their OSH awareness.

The duly completed questionnaire should be returned before or on 17-April-2012. Should there be any query, kindly contact and consult the undersigned via telephone numbers shown above.
Thank you very much

Yours sincerely,

(ANDREW ANAK RONGGIE)

Attachment – Brief Thesis Information and Questionnaire

We hereby agreed / disagree to grant you permission to carry out the abovesaid study amongst the fabrication workers /personnel in the Corporation's Yard. Thank you

Signature : ....
Name   : Puan Norhizan Sazali
Job Title   : Acting General Manager
Company : Brooke Dockyard and Engineering Works Corporation
Tel no.   : 082-439732 /082-439710

Research Information /Maklumat Kajian

Background	Latarbelakang
This academic research is conducted to examine the Occupational Safety and Health Induction Programme in enhancing safety awareness amongst fabrication workers. For that purpose, this study will be conducted within Brooke Dockyard and Engineering Works Corporation (BDEWC) focusing on employees whom involved directly or indirectly with fabrication works. There were two main research methodologies applied namely direct observation and personal survey using structured questionnaires form. A number of 175 employees are targeted as respondents which will cover the various sections within the above mentioned department. From the study findings, a number of recommendations will be suggested to be adopted inline to enhance the organization productivity with safer and healthier working environment and excellent safety culture.	Kajian penyelidikan ilmiah ini dijalankan untuk menilai keberkesanan program induksi (OSH in BM) dalam mewujudkan kesedaran keselamatan kerja dikalangan pekerja fabrikasi. Untuk tujuan kajian ini akan dilakukan di Brooke Dockyard and Engineering Works Corporation (BDEWC)dengan tumpuan terhadap pekerja yang terlibat secara langsung dan tidak langsung dengan kerja-kerja fabrikasi. Terdapat dua kaedah penyelidikan akan diaplikasikan untuk kajian ini iaitu pemerhatian secara terus dan tinjauan perseorangan menggunakan borang soal selidik. Seramai 175 pekerja disasarkan sebagai responden kajian ini yang merangkumi perlbgai seksyen atau unit dalam organisasi yang disebut diatas. Daripada hasil kajian, beberapa cadangan akan dikemukakan utuk diadaptasi selaras dengan matlamat untuk meningkatkan produktiviti organisasi dengan persekitaran kerja selamat dan budaya kerja selamat yang cemerlang.
Purpose of study The aim of this study is to examine OSH awareness level and knowledge amongst employees at Brooke Dockyard and to ensure that the Occupational Safety and Health Act 1994 and it regulation was followed by industries inline with promoting safe and healthy working environment and nurture OSH culture among employees.	**Tujuan Kajian** Kajian ini bertujuan untuk mengkaji tahap kesedaran dan pengetahuan OSH dikalangan pekerja di Limbongan Brooke dan untuk memastikan akta keselamatan dan kesihatan 1994 dan peraturan-peraturannya dipatuhi oleh pihak industry berhubung dengan mempromosikan persekitaran kerja yang sihat dan selamat serta memyemai budaya OSH dikalangan pekerja
The participants /Respondents a. Brooke Fabrication workers /personnel b. Subcontractors personnel c. Client Personnel d. Supplier /vendors personnel	**Peserta Kajian** a. Pekerja Limbongan Brooke b. Pekerja /Personnel Subkontraktor c. Pekerja /Personnel Klien d. Pembekal/Vendor
Study Procedures Fabrication workers who are respondents are required to: 1. Answer the questionnaire at the place of work 2. Fill in their particulars and respond to all the questions/statements.	**Prosidur Kajian** Pekerja yand juga responden dikehendaki untuk:- 1. Menjawab soalan-soalan at place of work 2. Mengisi butir-butir peribadi dan respon kepada semua soalan dan kenyataan.
Benefits of Study to the student - Learn the study processes - Enhance OSH knowledge - Produce Study Report - Contribute to the body of knowledge	**Faedah kajian kepada pelajar:** -Belajar proses pembelajaran -Menambah ilmu OSH -Menghasil laporan kajian yang boleh digunapakai -Menyumbang kepada badan ilmu pembelajaran
Possible drawbacks /Risks. There is no foreseeable risk in this study	**Risiko Penyertaan** *Kajian ini tidak mendatangkan sebarang risiko*
Researcher and Contact Numbers Andrew Anak Ronggie Off Tel : 082-432817 /HP:012-8085709	**Penyelidik dan yang boleh dihubungi** Andrew Anak Ronggie Off Tel : 082-432817 /HP:012-8085709

Appendix 3

Questionnaire

(English/Bahasa Melayu)

> **SURVEY OF
> HSE INDUCTION PROGRAM IN
> ENHANCING SAFETY AWARENESS AMONG
> FABRICATION WORKERS IN BROOKE
> DOCKYARD, KUCHING, SARAWAK**

You are kindly requested to spare a few minutes to help complete this questionnaire set. This survey is part of a research leading to an Executive Master's Degree.
So please note that your input is considered valuable to this survey and to be used for the academic purposely only.
Anda diminta untuk menluangkan beberapa minit untuk membantu melengkapkan borang soal selidik ini. Kaji selidik ini adalah sebahagian daripada penyelidikan yang membawa kepada Ijazah Sarjana Eksekutif. Jadi, sila ambil perhatian bahawa input anda dianggap penting untuk kajian ini dan akan hanya digunakan untuk latihan akademik sahaja.

Contact: Andrew Anak Ronggie (MD 091011)
Mobile: +60128085709

SECTION A: DEMOGRAPHIC BACKGROUND
LATARBELAKANG DEMOGRAFI

1. Age : _____ **years old**
Umur _____ *tahun*

2. Educational Level:/*Tahap Pendidikan***

a. No formal educational
Tiada asas pendidikan

b. Primary School
Sekolah Rendah

c. Secondary School
Sekolah Menengah

d. Tertiary level
Institute Pengajian Tinggi

3. Ethnic:*Etnik*

a. Malay/*Melayu*

b. Chinese/*China*

c. Iban/*Iban*

d. Bidayuh/*Bidayuh*

e. Others/*Lain-lain* _____

5. Job Title: _____

Jawatan: _____

6. Number of year(s) working experiences
with Brooke Dockyard: _____ years
Pengalaman bekerja dengan Brooke Dockyard: _____ *tahun*

7. Attended Course on OSH Induction?
Menghadiri kursus induksi OSH

a. Yes /*Ya* [When the latest/
Terkini : _____]

b. No/*Tidak*

8. Any experience accident at workplace (Brooke Dockyard)

a. Yes /*Ya* [When the latest/
Terkini : _____]

b. No/*Tidak*

4. Gender: a. Male b. Female
Jantina a. Lelaki b. Perempuan

SECTION B: Knowledge on OSH INDUCTION COURSE
PENGETAHUAN TENTANG KURSUS INDUKSI OSH

1. Who has been given responsibility for OSH within the organization?
Siapa yang telah diberi tanggungjawab untuk OSH dalam organisasi?

(a) OSH consultant   (b) Manager/Supervisor   (c) All employees

(a) Perunding OSH   *(b) Pengurus/Penyelia*   *(c) Semua pekerja*

2. Who can be fined under the act?
Siapakah yang boleh didenda di bawah Akta?

(a) Employees   (b) Employers   (c) Both employees and employers

| (A)Pekerja | (b) Majikan | (c) Kedua-dua pekerja dan majikan |

3. Regular inspections are vital to:
Pemeriksaan yang kerap adalah penting untuk:

| (a) identify hazards in the workplace | (b) keep the organization looking good | (c) aid communication |
| *(A) mengenal pasti bahaya di tempat kerja* | *(b) Memastikan organisasi kelihatan baik* | *(c) bantuan komunikasi* |

4. The responsibility to ensure a safe working environment lies with:
Tanggungjawab untuk memastikan persekitaran kerja yang selamat terletak dengan:

| (a) the property owner | (b) the employees | (c) the employer |
| *(A) pemilik harta* | *(b) pekerja* | *(c) majikan* |

5. The organization is:
Pertubuhan adalah:

| (a) an employer under workcover | (b) an exempt employer | (c) not insured |
| *(A) Penaung majikan* | *(b) majikan yang dikecualikan* | *(c) tidak diinsuranskan* |

6. If you had an OSH problem, you would first consult:
Jika anda mempunyai masalah OHS anda akan meminta nasihat:

| (a) your health and safety representative | (b) your supervisor | (c) the health and safety committee |
| *(A) Wakil Kesihatan dan Keselamatan anda* | *(b) Penyelia anda* | *(c) Jawatankuasa Kesihatan dan Keselamatan* |

7. In the event of a medical emergency, you would contact:
7. Sekiranya berlaku kecemasan perubatan, anda akan hubungi:

| (a) security | (b) your designated first-aid person | (c) OSH consultant |
| *(A) Pihak Keselamatan* | *(b) Individu yang ditetapkan untuk anda* | *(c) Perunding OSH* |

8. The Regular Inspection Checklist is located:
Senarai Semak Pemeriksaan berada:

| (a) Organization's Resource Centre | (b) HQ Services | (c) Organization Homepage |
| *(A) sumber Pusat Pertubuhan* | *(b) Ibu Pejabat Perkhidmatan* | *(c) Organisasi Laman Utama* |

9. MSDS stands for:

9. MSDS berdiri untuk:

(a) Material Safety
Delivery Sheet

(b) Medical Safety Data
Sheet

(c) Material Safety Data
Sheet

*(A) Risalah
Penghantaran
Keselamatan*

*(b) Risalah Data
Keselamatan Perubatan*

*(c) Data Keselamatan
Risalah*

10. When a hazard is identified, it is best practice to:

10. Apabila bahaya dikenal pasti terbaik mengamalkan:

(a) eliminate the hazard

(b) change work
practices

(c) use engineering or
administrative controls

*(A) menghapuskan
bahaya*

*(b) amalan kerja
perubahan*

*(c) kegunaan kejuruteraan
atau kawalan pentadbiran*

11. Using the risk assessment process, if an event is likely to occur with minor consequences, is the risk rated:

11. Menggunakan proses penilaian risiko, jika peristiwa yang mungkin berlaku dengan kecil, akibatnya, adalah risiko yang diberi nilai:

(a) low

(b) moderate

(c) high

(A) rendah

(b) sederhana

(c) tinggi

12. If a work process is identified as having some risk, and that risk cannot be eliminated or reduced, it is best to:

12. Jika proses kerja dikenalpasti sebagai mempunyai beberapa risiko dan risiko yang tidak boleh dihapuskan atau dikurangkan, cara yang terbaik adalah untuk:

(a) verbally inform
relevant staff

(b) e-mail relevant staff

(c) place safe operating
procedures where required

*(A) secara lisan
memberitahu kakitangan
yang berkaitan*

*(b) kakitangan e-mel
yang berkaitan*

*(c) prosedur operasi yang
selamat di mana perlu*

13. The next step following identifying and assessing a hazard is:

Berikut langkah seterusnya mengenal pasti dan menilai bahaya ialah:

(a) eliminating the
hazard

(b) controlling the
hazard

(c) notifying your supervisor

*(A) menghapuskan
bahaya*

(b) mengawal bahaya

*(c) memberitahu Penyelia
anda*

14. It would be best practice when dealing with a hazard to:

Ia akan menjadi amalan terbaik apabila berhadapan dengan bahaya kepada:

(a) identify appropriate PPE	(b) refer the issue to the OSH Committee	(c) follow the hierarchy of controls
(A) mengenal pasti alat perlindungan diri	*(b) merujuk isu itu kepada Jawatankuasa OHS*	*(c) mengikut hierarki kawalan*

15. A Code of Practice:
Kod Amalan:

(a) is mandatory	(b) provides information that may be followed	(c) is not relevant to the university
(A) adalah mandatori	*(b) menyediakan maklumat yang boleh diikuti*	*(c) tidak relevan kepada Universiti*

16. An employee shall:
Seorang pekerja hendaklah:

(a) protect his/her own safety at work	(b) obey any reasonable instructions in relation to OSH	(c) both (a) and (b)
(A) melindungi / menjamin keselamatan dirinya di tempat kerja	*(b) mematuhi apa-apa arahan yang munasabah berhubung dengan OHS*	*(c) kedua-dua (a) dan (b)*

17. When a regular inspection is completed, who takes remedial action?
Apabila Pemeriksaan Tetap selesai, yang mengambil tindakan pemulihan?

(a) OSH Consultant	(b) Head of School/ Manager of Unit	(c) the member(s) of staff identified in the inspection
(A) OSH Perunding	*(b) Ketua Sekolah / Pengurus Unit*	*(c) member (s) kakitangan yang dikenal pasti dalam pemeriksaan*

18. Supervisors must, in relation to OSH, provide staff with:
Penyelia perlu, berhubung dengan OSH, menyediakan kakitangan dengan:

(a) information, training and supervision	(b) a H&S representative	(c) reasonable working hours
(A) maklumat, latihan dan penyeliaan	*(b) Wakil H & S*	*(c) yang munasabah waktu kerja*

19. Accidents and incidents should be reported within:
Kemalangan dan kejadian yang perlu dilaporkan dalam tempoh:

(a) 24 hours	(b) 48 hours	(c) 5 working days
(A) 24 jam	*(b) 48 jam*	*(c) 5 hari bekerja*

20. Ergonomic assessment would aim to:

20. *Penilaian ergonomik bertujuan untuk:*

(a) identify suitable staff for the position	(b) correct poor posture and work practices to prevent injury	(c) identify OSH budget expenditure in the area
(A) mengenal pasti kakitangan yang sesuai bagi jawatan	*(b) postur yang betul miskin dan amalan kerja untuk mengelakkan kecederaan*	*(c) mengenal pasti OHS perbelanjaan bajet di kawasan*

FOR SECTION C TO E

Mark your answer by circling (¡) or tick (ü) a
number that represents your answer.
Only <u>one</u> answer for each question; give
answer that <u>best</u> describes yourself.
Do not mark on the words on top of numbers.

*1 = Strongly Disagree; 2=Disagree; 3=Undecided;
4=Agree; & 5=Strongly Agree*

SECTION C: Perception on Organization Safety Management	Answer
1. Provides enough safety programs / *Program Keselamatan yang mencukupi*	1.2.3.4.5
2. Conducts frequent safety inspection / *Kerap melakukan tinjauan keselamatan*	1.2.3.4.5
3. Investigates safety problems quickly / *Bertindak cepat mengatasi masalah*	1.2.3.4.5
4. Rewards safe workers / *Memberi ganjaran jika bekerja secara selamat*	1.2.3.4.5
5. Provides safe equipment / *Membekalkan peralatan keselamatan*	1.2.3.4.5
6. Provides safe working environments / *Menyediakan persekitaran kerja selamat*	1.2.3.4.5
7. Responds quickly to safety concerns / *Bertindak cepat terhadap isu berkaitan*	1.2.3.4.5
8. Helps maintain clean work area / *Membantu mengekalkan persekitaran bersih*	1.2.3.4.5

9. Provides safety information /
Membekalkan maklumat berkaitan keselamatan — 1.2.3.4.5

10. Keeps workers informed of hazards /
Memaklumkan ancaman bahaya — 1.2.3.4.5

SECTION D: Safety Programme/policies	Answer

1. Worthwhile /
Bermanfaat — 1.2.3.4.5

2. Helps prevent accident /
Membantu mencegah kemalangan — 1.2.3.4.5

3. Useful /
Berfaedah — 1.2.3.4.5

4. Good practices /
Amalan baik — 1.2.3.4.5

5. First-rate /
Paling Utama — 1.2.3.4.5

6. Clear & visionary /
Jelas & berwawasan — 1.2.3.4.5

7. Important /
Penting — 1.2.3.4.5

8. Effective in reducing injuries /
Berkesan mengurangkan kecederaan — 1.2.3.4.5

9. Must apply to my workplace /
Mesti diamalkan ditempat kerja — 1.2.3.4.5

10. Fully functioning /
Berfungsi sepenuhnya — 1.2.3.4.5

SECTION E: Perception on Safety Behavior at Workplace	Answer

1. Don't overlook safety procedures in order to get my job done more quickly.
Jangan mengabaikan keselamatan demi menyiapkan kerja dengan cepat. — 1.2.3.4.5

2. Follow all safety procedures regardless of the situation I am in.
Mematuhi prosedur keselamatan tanpa mengra situasi dihadap.i — 1.2.3.4.5

3. Handles all situations as if there is a possibility of having an accident.
Mengendalikan semua situasi mengandaikan berlaku kemalangan. — 1.2.3.4.5

4. Wear my safety equipment required by practice.
Menggunkan alat keselamatan mengikut ketatapan peraturan. — 1.2.3.4.5

5. Encourage my coworkers to be safe.
Menggalakkan rakansekerja untuk bekerja dengan selamat.   1.2.3.4.5

6. Keep my work equipment in safe working environment.
Memastikan kesemua peralatan kerja di dalam keadaan   1.2.3.4.5
selamat.

7. Do not take shortcuts in order to get my job done faster.
Elakkan jalan pintas untuk menyiapkan kerja dengan cepat.   1.2.3.4.5

8. Only follow safety rules that I think are necessary.
Hanya mematuhi peraturan yang difikirkan perlu   1.2.3.4.5

9. Report safety problems to my supervisor when I see
safety problems. *Melaporkan masalah keselamatan yang*   1.2.3.4.5
dilihat

10. Correct safety problems to ensure accidents will not
occur.
Menyelesaikan masalah keselamatan untuk mengelakkan   1.2.3.4.5
kemalangan

Appendix 4

Reliability Analysis

Scale: ALL VARIABLES

Reliability Statistics

Cronbach's Alpha	N of Items
.920	10

Item-Total Statistics

	Scale Mean if Item Deleted	Scale Variance if Item Deleted	Corrected Item-Total Correlation	Cronbach's Alpha if Item Deleted
Provides enough safety programs	39.96	26.576	.751	.909
Conducts frequent safety inspection	40.16	27.854	.675	.914
Investigates safety problems quickly	40.13	26.102	.694	.913
Rewards safe workers	40.04	26.646	.740	.910
Provides safe equipment	39.99	26.289	.748	.909
Provides safe working environments	40.04	27.871	.703	.913
Responds quickly to safety concerns	39.98	27.880	.701	.913
Helps maintain clean work area	40.18	28.262	.522	.922
Provides safety information	40.08	26.824	.689	.913
Keeps workers informed of hazards	39.96	26.153	.811	.906

Scale: ALL VARIABLES
Reliability Statistics

Cronbach's Alpha	N of Items
.939	10

Item-Total Statistics

	Scale Mean if Item Deleted	Scale Variance if Item Deleted	Corrected Item-Total Correlation	Cronbach's Alpha if Item Deleted
Worthwhile	39.78	30.795	.793	.931
Helps prevent accident	39.52	30.618	.791	.931
Useful	39.67	32.645	.659	.937
Good practices	39.66	32.534	.673	.937
First-rate	39.80	30.585	.785	.931
Clear & visionary	39.66	30.450	.774	.932
Important	39.73	30.689	.796	.931
Effective in reducing injuries	39.69	30.471	.774	.932
Must apply to my workplace	39.57	31.528	.758	.933
Fully functioning	39.67	31.800	.727	.934

Scale: ALL VARIABLES

Reliability Statistics	
Cronbach's Alpha	N of Items
.893	10

Item-Total Statistics

	Scale Mean if Item Deleted	Scale Variance if Item Deleted	Corrected Item-Total Correlation	Cronbach's Alpha if Item Deleted
Don't overlook safety procedures in order to get my job done more quickly.	37.68	30.544	.689	.878
Follow all safety procedures regardless of the situation I am in.	37.71	31.167	.723	.877
Handles all situations as if there is a possibility of having an accident.	37.84	31.220	.743	.876
Wear my safety equipment required by practice.	37.72	30.682	.745	.875
Encourage my coworkers to be safe.	37.79	31.195	.692	.879
Keep my work equipment in safe working environment.	37.69	30.834	.764	.874
Do not take shortcuts in order to get my job done faster.	37.67	31.053	.735	.876
Only follow safety rules that I think are necessary.	39.74	32.827	.205	.934
Report safety problems to my supervisor when I see safety problems. Melaporkan masalah keselamatan yang dilihat	37.84	30.840	.710	.877
Correct safety problems to ensure accidents will not occur.	37.58	30.485	.811	.872

Scale: ALL VARIABLES

Reliability Statistics

Cronbach's Alpha	N of Items
.965	30

Item-Total Statistics

	Scale Mean if Item Deleted	Scale Variance if Item Deleted	Corrected Item-Total Correlation	Cronbach's Alpha if Item Deleted
Provides enough safety programs	126.18	261.262	.802	.963
Conducts frequent safety inspection	126.38	266.633	.666	.963
Investigates safety problems quickly	126.36	261.231	.695	.963
Rewards safe workers	126.27	263.027	.728	.963
Provides safe equipment	126.22	261.495	.753	.963
Provides safe working environments	126.27	266.535	.698	.963
Responds quickly to safety concerns	126.20	267.191	.666	.963
Helps maintain clean work area	126.41	268.496	.504	.964
Provides safety information	126.31	263.750	.675	.963
Keeps workers informed of hazards	126.18	261.460	.794	.963
Worthwhile	126.42	262.147	.751	.963
Helps prevent accident	126.16	260.981	.777	.963
Useful	126.31	266.907	.641	.964
Good practices	126.31	266.384	.664	.963
First-rate	126.44	261.783	.735	.963
Clear & visionary	126.31	262.398	.689	.963
Important	126.38	261.307	.775	.963
Effective in reducing injuries	126.33	262.166	.700	.963
Must apply to my workplace	126.22	266.185	.630	.964
Fully functioning	126.31	267.259	.588	.964

Don't overlook safety procedures in order to get my job done more quickly.	126.27	260.563	.726	.963
Follow all safety procedures regardless of the situation I am in.	126.29	261.702	.785	.963
Handles all situations as if there is a possibility of having an accident.	126.43	262.021	.798	.963
Wear my safety equipment required by practice.	126.31	262.693	.709	.963
Encourage my coworkers to be safe.	126.38	261.547	.766	.963
Keep my work equipment in safe working environment.	126.28	261.118	.808	.962
Do not take shortcuts in order to get my job done faster.	126.26	261.292	.800	.963
Only follow safety rules that I think are necessary.	128.33	272.053	.173	.970
Report safety problems to my supervisor when I see safety problems. Melaporkan masalah keselamatan yang dilihat	126.43	263.584	.661	.963
Correct safety problems to ensure accidents will not occur.	126.17	262.070	.769	.963

Appendix 5

Knowledge Level on OSH Induction

Frequency Table

1. Who has been given responsibility for OSH within the organization?

		Frequency	Percent	Valid Percent	Cumulative Percent
Valid	OSH Consultant	12	8.4	8.4	8.4
	Manager/ Supervisor	28	19.6	19.6	28.0
	All employees	103	72.0	72.0	100.0
	Total	143	100.0	100.0	

2. Who can be fined under the act?

		Frequency	Percent	Valid Percent	Cumulative Percent
Valid	Employees	4	2.8	2.8	2.8
	Employers	32	22.4	22.4	25.2
	Both (employees and employers)	107	74.8	74.8	100.0
	Total	143	100.0	100.0	

3. Regular Inspections are vital to:

		Frequency	Percent	Valid Percent	Cumulative Percent
Valid	Identify hazards in the workplace	135	94.4	94.4	94.4
	Keep the organization looking good	6	4.2	4.2	98.6
	Aid communication	2	1.4	1.4	100.0
	Total	143	100.0	100.0	

4. The responsibility to ensure a safe working environment lies with:

		Frequency	Percent	Valid Percent	Cumulative Percent
Valid	The property owner	13	9.1	9.1	9.1
	The employees	64	44.8	44.8	53.8
	The employer	64	44.8	44.8	98.6
	4	2	1.4	1.4	100.0
	Total	143	100.0	100.0	

5. The organization is:

		Frequency	Percent	Valid Percent	Cumulative Percent
Valid	An employer under workcover	118	82.5	82.5	82.5
	An exempt employer	23	16.1	16.1	98.6
	4	2	1.4	1.4	100.0
	Total	143	100.0	100.0	

6. If you had an OSH problem, you would first consult:

		Frequency	Percent	Valid Percent	Cumulative Percent
Valid	Health and safety representative	87	60.8	60.8	60.8
	Supervisor	28	19.6	19.6	80.4
	The health and safety committee	28	19.6	19.6	100.0
	Total	143	100.0	100.0	

7. In the event of a medical emergency, you would contact:

		Frequency	Percent	Valid Percent	Cumulative Percent
Valid	Security	16	11.2	11.2	11.2
	Designated first-aid person	112	78.3	78.3	89.5
	OSH consultant	12	8.4	8.4	97.9
	Combined answer	3	2.1	2.1	100.0
	Total	143	100.0	100.0	

8. The Regular Inspection Checklist is located:

		Frequency	Percent	Valid Percent	Cumulative Percent
Valid	Organization Resource Centre	52	36.4	36.4	36.4
	HQ Services	59	41.3	41.3	77.6
	Organization Homepage	13	9.1	9.1	86.7
	Combined answer	19	13.3	13.3	100.0
	Total	143	100.0	100.0	

9. MSDS stands for:

		Frequency	Percent	Valid Percent	Cumulative Percent
Valid	Material Safety Delivery Sheet	8	5.6	5.6	5.6
	Medical Safety Data Sheet	31	21.7	21.7	27.3
	Material Safety Data Sheet	98	68.5	68.5	95.8
	Combined answer	6	4.2	4.2	100.0
	Total	143	100.0	100.0	

10. When a hazard is identified, it is best practice to:

		Frequency	Percent	Valid Percent	Cumulative Percent
Valid	Eliminate the hazard	79	55.2	55.2	55.2
	Change work practices	26	18.2	18.2	73.4
	Use engineering or administration controls	38	26.6	26.6	100.0
	Total	143	100.0	100.0	

11. Using the risk assessment process, if a event is likely to occur with minor consequence, is the risk rated:

		Frequency	Percent	Valid Percent	Cumulative Percent
Valid	Low	125	87.4	87.4	87.4
	Moderate	14	9.8	9.8	97.2
	High	4	2.8	2.8	100.0
	Total	143	100.0	100.0	

12. If a work process is identified as having some risk, and that risk cannot be eliminated or reduced, it is best to:

		Frequency	Percent	Valid Percent	Cumulative Percent
Valid	Verbally inform relevant staff	36	25.2	25.2	25.2
	E-mail relevant staff	4	2.8	2.8	28.0
	Place safe operation procedure where required	103	72.0	72.0	100.0
	Total	143	100.0	100.0	

13. The next step following identifying and assessing a hazard is:

		Frequency	Percent	Valid Percent	Cumulative Percent
Valid	Eliminating the hazard	39	27.3	27.3	27.3
	Controlling the hazard	87	60.8	60.8	88.1
	Notifying your supervisor	17	11.9	11.9	100.0
	Total	143	100.0	100.0	

14. It would be best practice when dealing with a hazard to:

		Frequency	Percent	Valid Percent	Cumulative Percent
Valid	Identify appropriate PPE	53	37.1	37.1	37.1
	Refer the issue to the OSS Committee	36	25.2	25.2	62.2
	Follow the hierarchy of control	54	37.8	37.8	100.0
	Total	143	100.0	100.0	

15. A Code of Practice:

		Frequency	Percent	Valid Percent	Cumulative Percent
Valid	Is mandatory	34	23.8	23.8	23.8
	Provides information that might be followed	107	74.8	74.8	98.6
	Is not relevant to the organization	2	1.4	1.4	100.0
	Total	143	100.0	100.0	

16. An employee shall:

		Frequency	Percent	Valid Percent	Cumulative Percent
Valid	Protect his/ her own safety at workplace	1	.7	.7	.7
	Obey any reasonable instructions in relation to OSH	4	2.8	2.8	3.5
	Both	138	96.5	96.5	100.0
	Total	143	100.0	100.0	

17. When a regular Inspection is completed, who takes remedial action?

		Frequency	Percent	Valid Percent	Cumulative Percent
Valid	OSH consultant	30	21.0	21.0	21.0
	Head of management unit	18	12.6	12.6	33.6
	The member(s) of staff identified the inspection	95	66.4	66.4	100.0
	Total	143	100.0	100.0	

18. Supervisors must, in relation to OSH, provide staff with:

		Frequency	Percent	Valid Percent	Cumulative Percent
Valid	Information, training, and supervision	141	98.6	98.6	98.6
	An H&S representative	2	1.4	1.4	100.0
	Total	143	100.0	100.0	

19. Accidents and incidents should be reported within:

		Frequency	Percent	Valid Percent	Cumulative Percent
Valid	24 hours	139	97.2	97.2	97.2
	48 hours	1	.7	.7	97.9
	5 working days	3	2.1	2.1	100.0
	Total	143	100.0	100.0	

20. Ergonomic assessment would aim to:

		Frequency	Percent	Valid Percent	Cumulative Percent
Valid	Identify suitable staff for the position	9	6.3	6.3	6.3
	Correct poor posture and work practices to prevent injury	127	88.8	88.8	95.1
	Identify OSH budget expenditure in the area	7	4.9	4.9	100.0
	Total	143	100.0	100.0	

Appendix 6

Study Constructs

Frequency Table

SECTION C: Perception on Organization Safety Management

		Frequency	Percent	Valid Percent	Cumulative Percent
Valid	Strongly Disagree	4	2.8	2.8	2.8
	Agree	47	32.9	32.9	35.7
	Strongly Agree	92	64.3	64.3	100.0
	Total	143	100.0	100.0	

Provides enough safety programs

		Frequency	Percent	Valid Percent	Cumulative Percent
Valid	Strongly Disagree	4	2.8	2.8	2.8
	Agree	49	34.3	34.3	37.1
	Strongly Agree	90	62.9	62.9	100.0
	Total	143	100.0	100.0	

Conducts frequent safety inspection

		Frequency	Percent	Valid Percent	Cumulative Percent
Valid	Disagree	4	2.8	2.8	2.8
	Undecided	4	2.8	2.8	5.6
	Agree	74	51.7	51.7	57.3
	Strongly Agree	61	42.7	42.7	100.0
	Total	143	100.0	100.0	

Investigates safety problems quickly

		Frequency	Percent	Valid Percent	Cumulative Percent
Valid	Strongly Disagree	4	2.8	2.8	2.8
	Disagree	4	2.8	2.8	5.6
	Undecided	2	1.4	1.4	7.0
	Agree	58	40.6	40.6	47.6
	Strongly Agree	75	52.4	52.4	100.0
	Total	143	100.0	100.0	

Rewards safe workers

		Frequency	Percent	Valid Percent	Cumulative Percent
Valid	Strongly Disagree	4	2.8	2.8	2.8
	Agree	61	42.7	42.7	45.5
	Strongly Agree	78	54.5	54.5	100.0
	Total	143	100.0	100.0	

Provides safe equipment

		Frequency	Percent	Valid Percent	Cumulative Percent
Valid	Strongly Disagree	4	2.8	2.8	2.8
	Undecided	4	2.8	2.8	5.6
	Agree	46	32.2	32.2	37.8
	Strongly Agree	89	62.2	62.2	100.0
	Total	143	100.0	100.0	

Provides safe working environments

		Frequency	Percent	Valid Percent	Cumulative Percent
Valid	Disagree	4	2.8	2.8	2.8
	Agree	65	45.5	45.5	48.3
	Strongly Agree	74	51.7	51.7	100.0
	Total	143	100.0	100.0	

Responds quickly to safety concerns

		Frequency	Percent	Valid Percent	Cumulative Percent
Valid	Disagree	4	2.8	2.8	2.8
	Agree	56	39.2	39.2	42.0
	Strongly Agree	83	58.0	58.0	100.0
	Total	143	100.0	100.0	

Helps maintains clean work area

		Frequency	Percent	Valid Percent	Cumulative Percent
Valid	Disagree	4	2.8	2.8	2.8
	Undecided	14	9.8	9.8	12.6
	Agree	57	39.9	39.9	52.4
	Strongly Agree	68	47.6	47.6	100.0
	Total	143	100.0	100.0	

Provides safety information

		Frequency	Percent	Valid Percent	Cumulative Percent
Valid	Strongly Disagree	4	2.8	2.8	2.8
	Undecided	3	2.1	2.1	4.9
	Agree	61	42.7	42.7	47.6
	Strongly Agree	75	52.4	52.4	100.0
	Total	143	100.0	100.0	

Keeps workers informed of hazards

		Frequency	Percent	Valid Percent	Cumulative Percent
Valid	Strongly Disagree	4	2.8	2.8	2.8
	Agree	49	34.3	34.3	37.1
	Strongly Agree	90	62.9	62.9	100.0
	Total	143	100.0	100.0	

SECTION D: Safety Programs/Policies

		Frequency	Percent	Valid Percent	Cumulative Percent
Valid	Strongly Disagree	4	2.8	2.8	2.8
	Undecided	4	2.8	2.8	5.6
	Agree	27	18.9	18.9	24.5
	Strongly Agree	108	75.5	75.5	100.0
	Total	143	100.0	100.0	

Worthwhile

		Frequency	Percent	Valid Percent	Cumulative Percent
Valid	Strongly Disagree	4	2.8	2.8	2.8
	Undecided	4	2.8	2.8	5.6
	Agree	75	52.4	52.4	58.0
	Strongly Agree	60	42.0	42.0	100.0
	Total	143	100.0	100.0	

Helps prevent accidents

		Frequency	Percent	Valid Percent	Cumulative Percent
Valid	Strongly Disagree	4	2.8	2.8	2.8
	Undecided	4	2.8	2.8	5.6
	Agree	38	26.6	26.6	32.2
	Strongly Agree	97	67.8	67.8	100.0
	Total	143	100.0	100.0	

Useful

		Frequency	Percent	Valid Percent	Cumulative Percent
Valid	Disagree	4	2.8	2.8	2.8
	Undecided	4	2.8	2.8	5.6
	Agree	64	44.8	44.8	50.3
	Strongly Agree	71	49.7	49.7	100.0
	Total	143	100.0	100.0	

Good practices

		Frequency	Percent	Valid Percent	Cumulative Percent
Valid	Disagree	4	2.8	2.8	2.8
	Undecided	4	2.8	2.8	5.6
	Agree	63	44.1	44.1	49.7
	Strongly Agree	72	50.3	50.3	100.0
	Total	143	100.0	100.0	

First-rate

		Frequency	Percent	Valid Percent	Cumulative Percent
Valid	Strongly Disagree	4	2.8	2.8	2.8
	Undecided	8	5.6	5.6	8.4
	Agree	70	49.0	49.0	57.3
	Strongly Agree	61	42.7	42.7	100.0
	Total	143	100.0	100.0	

Clear & visionary

		Frequency	Percent	Valid Percent	Cumulative Percent
Valid	Strongly Disagree	4	2.8	2.8	2.8
	Undecided	8	5.6	5.6	8.4
	Agree	51	35.7	35.7	44.1
	Strongly Agree	80	55.9	55.9	100.0
	Total	143	100.0	100.0	

Important

		Frequency	Percent	Valid Percent	Cumulative Percent
Valid	Strongly Disagree	4	2.8	2.8	2.8
	Undecided	4	2.8	2.8	5.6
	Agree	69	48.3	48.3	53.8
	Strongly Agree	66	46.2	46.2	100.0
	Total	143	100.0	100.0	

Effective in reducing injuries

		Frequency	Percent	Valid Percent	Cumulative Percent
Valid	Strongly Disagree	4	2.8	2.8	2.8
	Undecided	8	5.6	5.6	8.4
	Agree	54	37.8	37.8	46.2
	Strongly Agree	77	53.8	53.8	100.0
	Total	143	100.0	100.0	

Must apply to my workplace

		Frequency	Percent	Valid Percent	Cumulative Percent
Valid	Disagree	4	2.8	2.8	2.8
	Undecided	8	5.6	5.6	8.4
	Agree	42	29.4	29.4	37.8
	Strongly Agree	89	62.2	62.2	100.0
	Total	143	100.0	100.0	

Fully functioning

		Frequency	Percent	Valid Percent	Cumulative Percent
Valid	Disagree	4	2.8	2.8	2.8
	Undecided	8	5.6	5.6	8.4
	Agree	56	39.2	39.2	47.6
	Strongly Agree	75	52.4	52.4	100.0
	Total	143	100.0	100.0	

SECTION E: Perception on Safety Behavior at Workplace

		Frequency	Percent	Valid Percent	Cumulative Percent
Valid	Strongly Disagree	4	2.8	2.8	2.8
	Agree	96	67.1	67.1	69.9
	Strongly Agree	43	30.1	30.1	100.0
	Total	143	100.0	100.0	

Don't overlook safety procedures in order to get my job done more quickly.

		Frequency	Percent	Valid Percent	Cumulative Percent
Valid	Strongly Disagree	4	2.8	2.8	2.8
	Disagree	4	2.8	2.8	5.6
	Agree	49	34.3	34.3	39.9
	Strongly Agree	86	60.1	60.1	100.0
	Total	143	100.0	100.0	

Follow all safety procedures regardless of the situation I am in.

		Frequency	Percent	Valid Percent	Cumulative Percent
Valid	Strongly Disagree	4	2.8	2.8	2.8
	Agree	65	45.5	45.5	48.3
	Strongly Agree	74	51.7	51.7	100.0
	Total	143	100.0	100.0	

Handles all situations as if there is a possibility of having an accident.

		Frequency	Percent	Valid Percent	Cumulative Percent
Valid	Strongly Disagree	4	2.8	2.8	2.8
	Agree	84	58.7	58.7	61.5
	Strongly Agree	55	38.5	38.5	100.0
	Total	143	100.0	100.0	

Wear my safety equipment required by practice.

		Frequency	Percent	Valid Percent	Cumulative Percent
Valid	Strongly Disagree	4	2.8	2.8	2.8
	Undecided	4	2.8	2.8	5.6
	Agree	59	41.3	41.3	46.9
	Strongly Agree	76	53.1	53.1	100.0
	Total	143	100.0	100.0	

Encourage my coworkers to be safe.

		Frequency	Percent	Valid Percent	Cumulative Percent
Valid	Strongly Disagree	4	2.8	2.8	2.8
	Undecided	4	2.8	2.8	5.6
	Agree	69	48.3	48.3	53.8
	Strongly Agree	66	46.2	46.2	100.0
	Total	143	100.0	100.0	

Keep my work equipment in safe working environment.

		Frequency	Percent	Valid Percent	Cumulative Percent
Valid	Strongly Disagree	4	2.8	2.8	2.8
	Agree	63	44.1	44.1	46.9
	Strongly Agree	76	53.1	53.1	100.0
	Total	143	100.0	100.0	

Do not take shortcuts in order to get my job done faster.

		Frequency	Percent	Valid Percent	Cumulative Percent
Valid	Strongly Disagree	4	2.8	2.8	2.8
	Agree	60	42.0	42.0	44.8
	Strongly Agree	79	55.2	55.2	100.0
	Total	143	100.0	100.0	

Only follow safety rules that I think are necessary.

		Frequency	Percent	Valid Percent	Cumulative Percent
Valid	Strongly Disagree	50	35.0	35.0	35.0
	Disagree	35	24.5	24.5	59.4
	Undecided	26	18.2	18.2	77.6
	Agree	15	10.5	10.5	88.1
	Strongly Agree	17	11.9	11.9	100.0
	Total	143	100.0	100.0	

Report safety problems to my supervisor when I see safety problems.
Melaporkan masalah keselamatan yang dilihat

		Frequency	Percent	Valid Percent	Cumulative Percent
Valid	Strongly Disagree	4	2.8	2.8	2.8
	Undecided	8	5.6	5.6	8.4
	Agree	68	47.6	47.6	55.9
	Strongly Agree	63	44.1	44.1	100.0
	Total	143	100.0	100.0	

Correct safety problems to ensure accidents will not occur.

		Frequency	Percent	Valid Percent	Cumulative Percent
Valid	Strongly Disagree	4	2.8	2.8	2.8
	Agree	47	32.9	32.9	35.7
	Strongly Agree	92	64.3	64.3	100.0
	Total	143	100.0	100.0